OLD IRONSIDES

THE RISE, DECLINE, AND
RESURRECTION OF THE
USS *CONSTITUTION*

OLD IRONSIDES

THE RISE, DECLINE, AND RESURRECTION OF THE USS *CONSTITUTION*

Thomas C. Gillmer

INTERNATIONAL MARINE

CAMDEN, MAINE

International Marine/
Ragged Mountain Press

A Division of The **McGraw-Hill** Companies

4 6 8 10 9 7 5 3

Library of Congress Cataloging-in-Publication Data

Gillmer, Thomas C.
Old ironsides: the rise, decline, and resurrection of the USS
Constitution / Thomas C. Gillmer.
p.   cm.
Includes bibliographical references and index.
ISBN 0-07-024564-9
1. Constitution (Frigate)—History. 2. United States—History.
Naval—To 1900. I. Title.
VA65.C7G55   1993
359.3'225—dc20   93-27934
CIP

Questions regarding the content of this book should be addressed to:
International Marine
P.O. Box 220
Camden, ME 04843

Questions regarding the ordering of this book should be addressed to:
The McGraw-Hill Companies
Customer Service Department
P.O. Box 547
Blacklick, OH 43004
Retail Customers: 1-800-262-4729
Bookstores: 1-800-722-4726

Old Ironsides is printed on acid-free paper.

Printed by Quebecor Printing Company, Fairfield, PA
Design by James Brisson
Production by Janet Robbins
Typeset by Farrar Associates
Edited by J.R. Babb, Jane Crosen, Michael Brosnan

To Joshua Humphreys,
the creator of the frigate
Constitution concept.

CONTENTS

ACKNOWLEDGMENTS

It may seem presumptuous for one whose experience is centered in engineering science rather than history to write about a subject so prominent in American history. However, when you recognize that the subject—a singular frigate original to our embryonic Navy—is now reaching the end of her second centennial, her continued life must be seen as an engineering problem.

Much has been written about "Old Ironsides," but nothing that I have seen has dealt with her structural problems, other than a few scholarly papers in technical journals. Therefore, I have combined here a recital of her historic life as a ship of our early and growing Navy with an assessment of her structure today. This, I believe, will help you to understand how she has evolved from her strenuous early life, through a long period of indifference, indecision, sporadic repairs, and restorations, to her present condition.

In this book I have relied on many sources, predominantly from government archives and literature. Beyond the National Archives and the Navy

Department, whose personnel from "Ship's Structures" I gratefully acknowledge, was a specific document of reference, *The USS* Constitution *Maintenance Manual*, prepared and assembled by Peter W. Witherell and published by the Naval Sea Systems Command, U.S. Navy. This manual is a tome of data from original sources telling what has been done with this great ship—and, between the lines, what has not been done. One of the most significant contributors to Witherell's maintenance manual is Commander Tyrone G. Martin, USN (Ret), a commanding officer of USS *Constitution* from 1974 to 1978. His book, *A Most Fortunate Ship*, is perhaps the most thoroughly detailed account of *Constitution*'s daily life and personnel.

In the collection of material, namely the illustrations, I am indebted to my good friend and superlative marine artist William Gilkerson. Bill is more than an artist; he is a particularly gifted scholar of maritime history of the 18th and 19th centuries, with special regard to ships.

The U.S. Naval Academy Museum also holds a valuable store of graphics involving *Constitution* and her contemporaries. I thank the curator of the Beverley R. Robinson Collection, Sigrid Trumpy, for enabling me to draw upon this source of naval art.

The assembly and processing of material for publication involves countless people-hours, the patient work of skilled hands and understanding minds. My draftsman, Iver Franzen, rendered most of the finished drawings from some of the original plans of *Constitution*, and many of these are new exposures of *Constitution*'s characteristics. The tireless work of transforming all the words into publishable copy must surely and gratefully be recognized as that of Jane Stuchell, my secretary.

PREFACE

This is the story of the USS *Constitution*, the most famous and successful of the early United States warships—and the oldest still afloat. This book is not about the heroics of famous old Navy captains who took her into history. It's about the ship herself, about her design, her style, her structure and strengths—and, finally, how I believe she can best be restored and preserved for generations to come.

My involvement with *Constitution* began two years ago when the Director of Ship's Structures in the Navy Department (under Naval Sea Systems Command) called to ask if his department could retain my services to make a structural study of *Constitution*. In addition to being a national monument, *Constitution* is still on the Navy list—in commission, with a regular crew and commanding officer. I accepted the invitation, and for about six months I concentrated on the ship's present structure and her structural history, studying the great body of records and documents on and about *Constitution*—of which there are perhaps more than on any other naval vessel. The Navy Ship's Structures office also wanted recommendations for correcting the ship's various infirmities of age, and to suggest restoration procedures that would help her survive the next 50 years. The results of this study and recommendations are summarized in the final chapters.

As every schoolchild should know, the frigate *Constitution* is approaching her 200th birthday. Launched in 1797, this grand ship, together with two sisterships, was the largest American warship of the day. She was a frigate, analogous to a cruiser of today, and, at 44 guns, was considered by European naval powers, particularly the British, to be an especially heavy member of her class. Swift, powerful frigates were deemed the best compromise sea defense for a fledgling navy and country. Who could stand against the British Empire and their thousand-ship Navy? Of their great floating fortresses, or ships-of-the-line, the largest, or "first rates," each carried more than 100 guns. In 1804 the British had ten first rates—altogether 190 ships-of-the-line carrying 74 or more guns each, as well as some 220 fourth- and fifth-rate ships, similar to *Constitution*.

To defend the new republic, Congress authorized a series of six frigates in 1794, and the size, shape, and structure of these was left largely in the hands of one man, Joshua Humphreys. Of this original U.S. Navy, the sole survivor, affectionately called "Old Ironsides," is *Constitution*.

A running contradiction to *Constitution*'s unique distinction of being the oldest and only surviving frigate anywhere has been presented by the friends of an old ship now attached to Baltimore's downtown Harborfront, identified as the U.S. frigate *Constellation*. The six frigates originally authorized in 1794 were three of 44 guns, one of which was *Constitution*, and three of 36 guns, including one named *Constellation*. Of the first six frigates, the latter was first to be completed and sailed—an honorable and singular distinction; however, the vessel now in Baltimore is not that ship, but a U.S. warship of the same name built in the Norfolk Navy Yard in 1855. I will briefly expand on that story in later pages.

Constitution's sides are not really made of iron, but during the War of 1812, when cannon shot bounced repeatedly off her sides, they certainly seemed to be. She was a tough and handsome warship then. She is still tough today, and could be restored to a close likeness of the way she looked during her youth. Who among us would not want that ourselves?

Thomas C. Gillmer
Annapolis, 1993

The First U.S. Naval Establishment

She was beautiful in her youth. Her fine lines and graceful sheer, her slightly scrolled and upturned head, the classic quarter galleries and restrained carvings gracing her 18th-century transom stern—all flowed together flawlessly in this magnificent creature of the sea. Her lofty rig spread more sail than any European frigate. In fact, she was larger in every way than most of her contemporary kind. The British Royal Navy saw her not as a frigate, but as a ship stronger than any of its fifth-rate ships-of-the-line.

To understand what is meant by the term "fifth rate," and where *Constitution* and her sisters fit into the naval categories of power of the day, let's take a brief look at the British rating system. In the first decade of the 19th century the British had more warships than any other country—so many large and formidable sailing fortresses that they proudly rated them according to size and power.

Ratings of these heavy ships were determined by a combination of firepower and size, which, of course, were interdependent. A first rate was a ship with three gun decks; this did not include the exposed weather deck, which carried carronades. With 32-pounders on the lowest deck, 24-

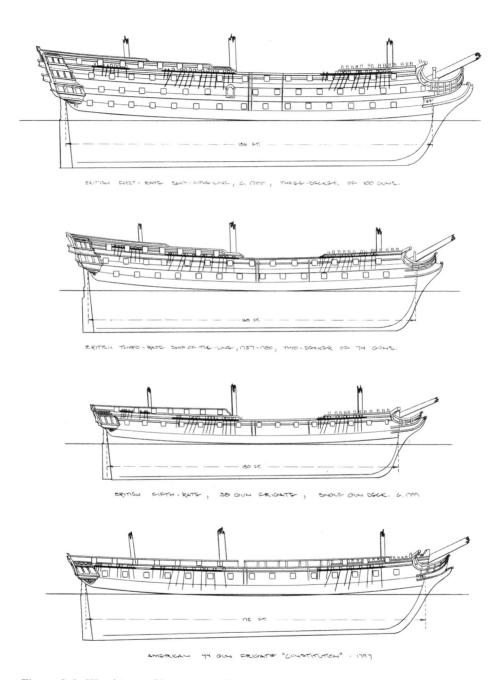

BRITISH FIRST-RATE SHIP OF THE LINE, c. 1788, THREE-DECKER OF 100 GUNS.

BRITISH THIRD-RATE SHIP OF THE LINE, 1757-1780, TWO-DECKER OF 74 GUNS.

BRITISH FIFTH-RATE, 38 GUN FRIGATE, SINGLE GUN DECK c. 1799

AMERICAN 44 GUN FRIGATE "CONSTITUTION" · 1797

Figure 1-1. Warship profiles typical of the early 19th century and contemporary with *Constitution*, all drawn to the same scale. Gunpower as well as sailing performance contributed to a ship's effectiveness.

pounders on the middle deck, and 18-pounders on the upper gun deck, plus carronades, a first-rate ship mounted 100 to 120 guns.[1] At 190 to 200 feet in length and up to 2,000 tonnage capacity by 1804, the first rate—of which there were ten in the Royal Navy—was larger and heavier than any other kind of warship, and more unwieldy. The famous HMS *Victory*, Lord Nelson's flagship at Trafalgar (1805), was a first-rate ship-of-the-line built in 1783.

The second rates were slightly less imposing than the first rates, with between 80 and 100 guns of similar size on three gun decks, and of generally less than 2,000 tonnage. Because they lacked the impressive power of the first rates and were relatively poor sailers, being high-sided for their shorter length, these ships were not especially popular. In 1804, 37 second rates were listed in the Royal Navy—many of these from earlier years.

The third rates mounted fewer than 80 guns, on two gun decks. The most popular third rate was the famous 74-gun ship, an ideal compromise among firepower, speed, and agility, and considered the most useful in the line of battle. In 1804, the Royal Navy listed 94 of these ships. The 74s carried 24-pounders, generally on their gun decks. The largest of these 74s were about 180 feet on deck. The smallest of the third rates was a 64-gun ship, generally considered a bargain-basement 74—yet in 1812 the British had 41 of them, many held over from the 18th century.

Fourth-rate ships were two-deckers of 50 to 60 guns. The 50s were considered too small for the battle line, but toward the end of the 18th century they were revived for duty as patrol and squadron-command ships. They were virtually the same as frigates, although their guns were distributed on two gun decks below the weather deck. Nineteen were on the British list in 1793.

Finally, there were the fifth-rate ships: frigates carried fewer than 50 guns and but one gun deck, but always gunned on the spar deck. In 1812, the British had 63 of the 36-gun frigates, the most popular of the fifth-rate ships. It also had 16 of the 38-gun frigates built between 1801 and 1812, as well as a number of 44s. These frigates weren't strong enough to stand up ship for ship with the new heavy 44-gun frigates of the young American

Navy. But they were versatile and could be used for patrolling, cruising, blockading, convoying, and apprehending smugglers.

In addition, the British Navy had also converted many captured foreign frigates, particularly French frigates, which it used to round out its fleet in the early 1800s. The largest of these were 40- to 44-gun frigates—a decent size, but not the most durable, since they were generally constructed of pine or other fast growing wood, rather than of English oak.

Altogether, in 1812, when USS *Constitution* sailed in her most successful year of the naval war against Great Britain, the British Royal Navy consisted of 1,017 warships of all classes. The United States Navy counted 18, none larger than *Constitution*.

I make this brief diversion into the types and styles of British warships at the beginning of the 19th century to point out the ridiculous disparity between the naval establishments of Great Britain and the struggling states of America. The states were united mostly in name, and at the turn of the century they suffered collectively the indignities of British arrogance toward the wayward colonies.

To provide ship crews for the Royal Navy, which was embroiled in an interminable war of attrition with France under Napoleon, the Admiralty relied on impressment. The press gangs made routine excursions into waterfront establishments—pubs and taverns, even conveniently located homes—to "recruit" their crewmen. Merchant vessels at sea, however, were an even more convenient source of experienced sailors. That American ships carried sailors speaking the same language, who still bore the taint of rebellion, made American-flagged ships a special target.

In the late 18th and early 19th century the American merchant marine tried desperately to establish reliable foreign trade relations. The coastal and developing inland states of the poverty-stricken union depended almost entirely upon the continuity of selling export commodities abroad: tobacco, flour, timber, salted fish, sugar, cotton, even newly built ships. This was a precarious life-support system, especially since Europe was at war.

America's expanding merchant fleet of modest but well-built ships was manned by well-paid American crews wary of being snatched away by Royal

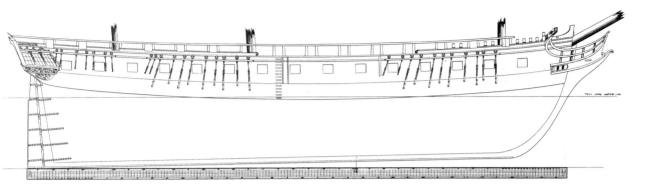

Figure 1-2. This bare profile drawing, based on the original draft by William Doughty, shows the U.S. frigate *Constitution* as she was designed by Joshua Humphreys, built and under construction from 1795 and launched in October 1797. It is highly likely that this was her appearance when launched.

Navy boarding gangs. Admittedly the attraction of becoming an American sailor had encouraged many a British tar to desert his native land and ship and join an American crew. The British considered this adequate justification to board American vessels whenever found and take off suspected deserters—some of whom were deserters, but many of whom were native-born Americans. Such were the bullying tactics of a vastly superior force.

A New Navy

Four years after the Battle of Yorktown and the cessation of revolutionary hostilities with the British Empire, America found herself without a single armed vessel to protect her hard-won sovereignty. By 1785 she had sold off the few that remained from the war. It was not until March 1794 that, after suffering the further humiliation of paying tribute to Mediterranean pirates, Congress reluctantly passed an act to create a naval force, and authorized the construction of six large frigates.

They were to be:

Constitution	44 guns, 1,576 tons, built at Boston
President	44 guns, 1,576 tons, built at New York
United States	44 guns, 1,576 tons, built at Philadelphia
Chesapeake	36 guns, 1,244 tons, built at Norfolk
Congress	36 guns, 1,286 tons, built at Portsmouth
Constellation	38 guns, 1,265 tons, built at Baltimore

Captains and officers for these vessels were commissioned and appointed by June 1794, and the Secretary of War (there being no Secretary of the Navy as yet) as early as April had named naval constructors, then instructing them to proceed with the designs and prepare for construction.

Joshua Humphreys, of Philadelphia, a Quaker shipbuilder with considerable shipbuilding experience as well as considerable influence in political circles, was appointed overall supervisor of construction of these first federal frigates. In addition to the six Congressionally authorized vessels, within a year or two some of the larger cities of the young country were building frigates and smaller warships to contribute to the young navy. The most significant of these "subscription" frigates were *Essex*, 32 guns; *John Adams*, 28 guns; *Philadelphia*, 38 guns; and *New York*, 36 guns.

It was Humphreys who created the concept for the original six frigates. Although he most likely did not draft the final plans, it was his theory—also supported by Henry Knox, the Secretary of War—that the necessarily small navy must be cored by able, hard-hitting frigates with good sailing performance. Larger than most British frigates, faster, and with greater cruising capability and harder-hitting gunnery, they would be able to run away from an overwhelming force of greater warships and stand and fight anything of approximate power.

Humphreys rightly discarded the idea of building larger two-deckers, such as the popular 74s, which were relatively quick and hard-hitting but did not have the lower profile and overall superior sailing performance of a frigate. The new frigates had to be capable of the immediate task of discouraging the Muslim pirates in the Mediterranean. For long-range naval duties, they had to be capable, if necessary, of independent wartime commerce-raiding cruises.

This philosophy was good, although Humphreys would live to see some flaws in his basic thinking. As told in Chapter Two, *Constitution* would find herself in the company of an enemy squadron, with no sailing breeze; she consequently fell into a towing match, with the smaller, lighter British frigates having the advantage. *Constitution* finally escaped by making good use of the trick of anchor kedging and a fortuitous rain squall and a curtain of darkness.

My intent is not to belittle sailing performance in the design of a frigate or any other type of sailing vessel. In ship design, balancing sailing performance with effective power is tricky business. What any 18th-century shipbuilder hoped for was a design that provided optimum power and speed for a ship to win duels against ships of equal size, while providing enough speed to escape more heavily gunned ships. In this regard, Joshua Humphreys's *Constitution*-class frigates proved their worth more than once, especially in foul weather when adequate freeboard allowed the heavy gun ports to remain open without the ship losing any sailing performance.

In the 18th century, the art of naval architecture was just beginning to become a science. The disclosure of metacentric principles, first recognized and applied in France and in French warships, had brought about the theory of ship stability. In the 1760s, Pierre Bougher, while employed by his government to measure the circumference of the Earth at the equator, found himself often on board ship in tropical seas. The discomfort of constant rolling stimulated his scientific mind to probe the causes of ship motion, and the result was the *theory of the metacenter*. This happened nearly simultaneously with the birth of the metric system, but without any tangible relation. The new theory emphasized the great importance of a lower center of gravity in a ship. For existing ships, it meant that the cargo needed to be loaded in a way that kept the center of gravity as low as possible and that the heavier guns were placed on the lowest gun deck.

It is doubtful that by 1794 any of this theoretical knowledge had filtered through the shipbuilding profession. But ship designers were clearly aware of the value of a lower center of gravity since freeboard was being reduced uniformly, even among the British and French first-rate three-deckers.

Not until more than half a century later did the experiments of English hydrodynamist William Froude reveal another area of concern: the nature of ship resistance. One of the components of the resistance in moving a ship through the water, he observed, was the apparent wave-like disturbance. These were self-generated waves, obviously representing consumption of energy, and as the speed of the vessel increased, the waves increased in height and length. At the same time, Froude reasoned that there was another important component of propulsion energy: the frictional drag of water moving over the hull's wetted surface. A slowly moving vessel's total resistance was due mostly to this frictional drag, which increases linearly with speed, while the wave-making drag increases exponentially. Overcoming these basic energy requirements was, then, the necessary power output of the wind on the sails. These observations were given mathematical formulations and recognized as Froude's Laws in 1874.

It is unlikely that naval architects and shipbuilders at the turn of the 19th century were thinking in these abstract terms, but the slow and relentless power of empirical thought was progressing in that direction. Even in the backwaters of the Chesapeake Bay, builders of the small, local schooners of 150 tons or so recognized that, for a fast-sailing hull, a sharp entrance was of key importance. The Chesapeake Bay builders also knew, perhaps instinctively or by observation, that a hull with accentuated deadrise and flat quarters combined with a sharp entrance made for excellent sailing performance. Whether they also observed that such a hull slipped through the water with little, if any, noticeable disturbance to the water's surface is immaterial.

Some of these sharp-built Chesapeake schooners were ordered by the U.S. Navy. Examples are *Experiment* and *Enterprise*, built in 1799 on Maryland's eastern shore. These were types of the famous Baltimore Clippers—which is, of course, another story, recounted in my *Pride of Baltimore: The Story of the Baltimore Clippers* (International Marine, 1992).

The hulls of these first six federal frigates were obviously designed by an experienced and well-trained hand aware of the basics of hydrodynamics. The entrances were not overly bluff, the lower stems were raked in a nicely rounded cutaway, the keels were trimmed down aft, and the quarters were reasonably flat. But, for competitive sailing, the hulls were not extreme enough to take advantage of the yet-unknown Froude's Laws. Humphreys's concept resulted in high-displacement, deep-draft hulls that would pull a wave astern of them. Altogether they were not the ultimate in performance, they represented a large improvement over their ancestral designs and were decisively better than the hulls of potential enemy ships abroad.

The six frigates were almost all designed to the same mold, with two categories of weight. The three 44-gun *Constitution*-class ships—*Constitution*, *President*, and *United States*—were the heaviest. They measured approximately 175 feet down the length of the gun deck, which is much the same as the length between perpendiculars or stemhead to sternpost at the rabbets. Their maximum beam or breadth to the inside of the planking (molded dimension) was 43½ feet. Their displacement, unladen, was 1,576 tons; loaded, approximately 2,200 tons. The dimensions of the 36-gun frigates of the *Constellation* class—*Constellation*, *Congress*, and *Chesapeake*—will have to remain irrelevant at this point.

The concept, and the question of design

The specific origins and final drafting of the heavy frigate's design are fogged over by time, loss of records, and contention, and it is not my purpose to be further contentious.

What is clear is that Joshua Humphreys, nominally the ship constructor responsible for design and construction, was assisted in design by a very capable and knowledgeable naval architect, Josiah Fox, who had arrived in America from England only a few years before the frigates were authorized. It is said he came in 1787 on a tour or sojourn, looking at American sources of ship timber. A young man about 30, Fox had received his training in the Royal Navy Dockyard at Plymouth. He was not only a skilled draftsman, but was also acquainted with the most modern naval architectural theory of the period. In addition to becoming educated, this young man had broadened his knowledge, having visited, before coming to America, many shipyards on the European continent, including the then-great Arsenal in Venice. Fox, soon assigned by Henry Knox to assist Humphreys, decided to stay in America. He was, like Humphreys, a Quaker and no doubt found Philadelphia an agreeable climate. He was also reasonably well connected, being a cousin of Surveyor General Andrew Ellicott and a family friend of a Navy captain, John Barry.

After an applicant examination, Fox was accepted as a temporary administrative assistant to the Secretary of War. His first duties were to help in the design of the newly authorized frigates, and he proceeded to the drawing board to draft a design for a 44-gun frigate. Joshua Humphreys, in the meantime, having his own concept of the new frigates, had prepared a model; we must speculate that this was one of the conventional half models which for many years was the practice of shipbuilders prior to construction.

Both of these proposals were submitted to the War Department. It is interesting to compare the two men's approaches: one a three-dimensional model, the other an orthographic drawing. These two differing expressions might be a comment on the respective age difference between Humphreys and Fox or even evidence of a change in the approach to ship design—a point of technological progress for American shipbuilding.

It would be nice to believe that the War Department selected one of these two proposals, but that apparently was not to be. Upon critical judgment by a third party, John Wharton (Humphreys's former partner in the Philadelphia shipyard)—together with subsequent discussions among Humphreys, Fox, and the War Department—both proposals were returned for modification and a single agreeable design.

Most naval architects do not agree that a conceptual or even a preliminary design is possible "by committee"; there must be a decision-maker, a central mind in the process. In this case, however, no records, letters, or other documents have survived to tell us who determined the final building design of USS *Constitution*, *United States*, or *President*—or, for that matter, any of the three smaller frigates of the *Constellation* class.

We know, however, that all of the hull designs are of the same character. Two original drawings of *Constitution* exist: one signed by Humphreys's chief draftsman, William Doughty (Figure 1-3) and one signed by Josiah Fox (Figure 1-4). These two separate design drawings—showing the sheer profile, the waterlines, and the body plan—are similar except for small characteristics (Figures 1-4 and 1-5). There are no design drawings of the ships signed by Joshua Humphreys.

Nonetheless, Humphreys clearly was *Constitution*'s conceptual designer. He, like many naval architects before and since, relied on the skill of his chief draftsman, in this case William Doughty, to express his concepts in the then new medium of orthographic projection.

(When naval architects, then and today, employ draftsmen, the employer and not the draftsman is rightly identified as the *designer*. The draftsman often signs his work as in the existing draft of *Constitution*. In fact, on this original draft signed "William Doughty, 1794" there is also a note in the upper left under the table of dimensions "original by Joshua Humphreys of Philadelphia." Whether this is his actual signature or a note of identity is not clear.)

Humphreys decided what these first handsome frigates should look like, what their dimensions should be, and what armament they should carry. Also, there is no doubt that, in the refinement of these warship designs, he had profited by Josiah Fox's knowledgeable input. From some of the surviving correspondence between Fox and Humphreys, we can clearly see some understandable impatience with the design process, as Humphreys kept pushing Fox to speed up the offsets and begin the lofting process. (This sort of work, for any philosophically motivated designer, is pure tedium.) Doubtless there was some friction working between these two men.

Little is said of the third party in the creative process, William Doughty.

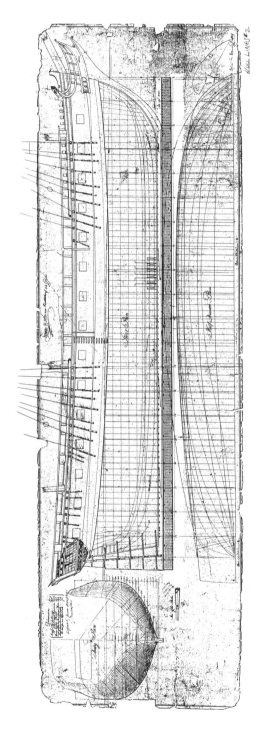

Figure 1-3. This beautifully drafted 1794 drawing, signed by William Doughty (draftsman of Joshua Humphreys), shows the original hull lines of sister frigates *Constitution* and *United States*, built in 1797.

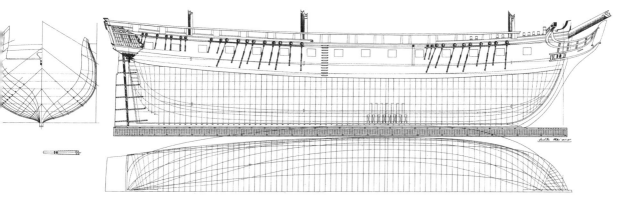

Figure 1-4. The hull lines of *Constitution* as drawn in 1795 by Josiah Fox, an English naval architect employed by the U.S. War Department to assist Joshua Humphreys. These lines are similar to Doughty's draft, but are not identical.

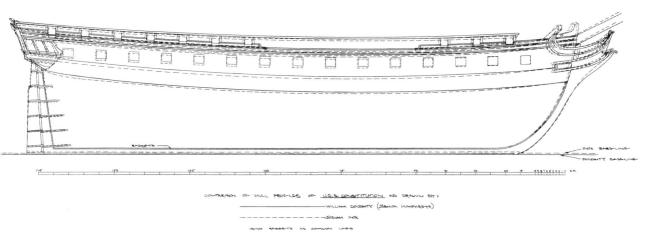

Figure 1-5. A superimposition of the Fox hull profile (dashed lines) on top of that by William Doughty (solid lines), using the keel rabbet as a common baseline, compares the two design drafts. Doughty's lines show a greater freeboard and less sheer. The dimensions where they may be still comparable on the actual ship favor Doughty's design.

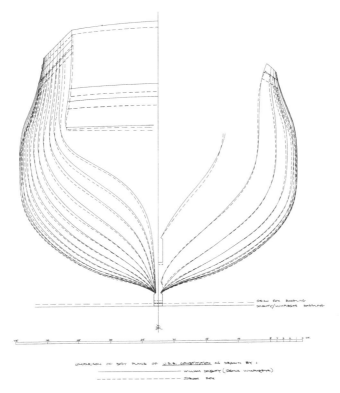

Figure 1-6. The overlay of Fox's body plan sections on those drawn by Doughty illustrates the variations of curvature in the sides and bottom. The most significant departures show in the after quarters where Fox created a fuller after body. Doughty's fuller topsides show in the tumblehome, both forward and aft. Surely these are not the same ship—neither in displacement nor in linear form.

While being the more silent party, Doughty was a skilled and upwardly mobile master ship's draftsman. His design drawings, not only of *Constitution* but of many other vessels, speak for his skill and creativity. He went on to become the Navy's Chief Naval Constructor from 1813 through the 24 years to follow.

An unbiased and appreciative naval architect in today's computer world cannot help but be astounded at the quality manual draftsmanship of these late-18th-century naval architects. The fineness and fairness of line, the grace and art in detail, the nearly perfect projections in three views—this sort of technical craftsmanship has long disappeared from marine drawings. The *lines draft*, the central focus and master delineation of a ship's hull in three projections, determines the shape of a hull, its speed through the water, its ability to go to windward, its carrying capacity, its seakindliness, and to a significant degree its stability and safety in a seaway. The lines drawing is a summary of the ship's most important characteristics and the foundation upon which all other drawings must rest.

At the National Archives in Washington, one can still examine the original drawings of *Constitution* by both Fox and Doughty. On both drawings, the draftsmanship is masterful, professional work.

Seeing the ship in the design

Aside from the remarkable draftsmanship of the design drawings, we must look through these finely drawn lines and see the ship, impressively displayed in three dimensions. The profile is most striking, showing the beauty of lifting sheer in the bow and stern. The stern, particularly, with its elegant but not overdone quarter galleries, shows the nice rise of the round tuck stern, shaping the run of the hull's bottom and into the terminus of its mainwale. The bow, with graceful stem knees, extends to meet the cutwater's upward and curving profile. The lower molding of the stem knee ends at the forward extremity as a simple scrolled base for a figurehead. The figurehead is not shown partly because it is not a responsibility of the designer. A specially assigned carver-sculptor is contracted separately for this. As will be seen later, the figurehead design can be quite controversial. The absence of the figurehead in this case, I believe, renders the forward profile of this design more beautiful.

The spar deck, as drawn in the design drafts, has no closed gunwale, but instead has been left open, enclosed only by a continuous railing on stanchions that define gun emplacements. This heavy guardrail terminates forward abreast of the foremast, and the line of the railcap does not follow the ship's true sheerline, lending the illusion of a flatter profile. It is believed that shortly after commissioning, or possibly during construction, the after section of open rail from the mainmast aft was closed in by a solid gunwale; this appears as such in the earliest of artist's renderings. Also, the space enclosed by the head rails, which fall gracefully from below the catheads and curve back up to terminate and form the backrest for a

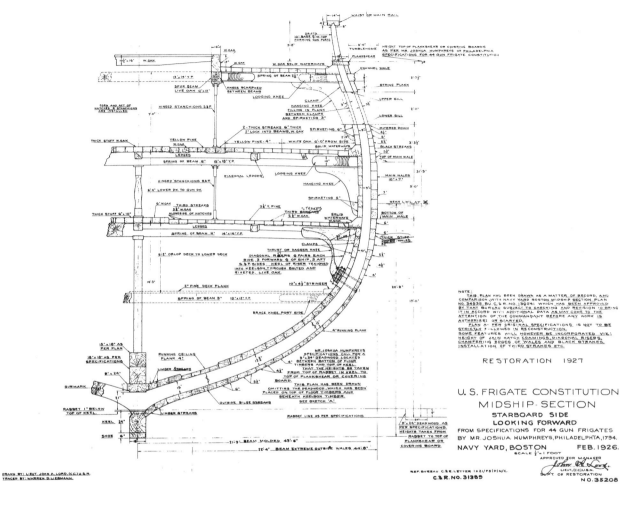

Figure 1-7. This structural transverse mid-section is believed to be very close to *Constitution*'s original construction requirements. Although it was drawn by Lieutenant John Lord in 1926 before his extensive restoration, it is based on Joshua Humphreys' original specifications of 1794. Note how the thickness of the outside planking and the inner ceiling vary nearly inversely from the keel to the upper deck.

figurehead below the bowsprit, was apparently tampered with during the ship's subsequent years. Ultimately, it became the ugly, boxy enclosure of the head which has persisted until this day. These and other changes wrought by maintenance, alterations, and repairs ordered by captains and others—in their zeal to "improve" or change things to their own sense of utility and dimension—have, over time, robbed the ship of much of her original beauty. These changes become very visible in the illustrations in Chapters Three, Four, and Five.

These early drafts by Doughty and Fox that agree so well also show the body plan. This original design form has held its characteristic shape reasonably well over time. *Constitution*, in her latest measurements, shows some inevitable, gradual, middle-age spread of about 1.2 feet amidships as well as an unmeasured drop in her bilges. The ship's notable deadrise in a "hollow" garboard shape reflects an early desire by the designer for sailing performance. These hollow garboards still exist, and perhaps are more pronounced.

The waterlines in the half-breadth plan flow easily and gently aft to a finely tapered ending; their shape forward is noticeably lacking in the bluffness traditional to the old warships. It can be quickly seen that the maximum breadth is substantially forward of amidships; this occurs (maximum section) at a point less than 70 feet aft of the stem. The idea of carrying the fullness of the hull's body forward of amidships is a carry-over of the old idea that began among 16th-century English shipwrights, who referred to this shape as "cod's head and mackerel's tail." There is no hydrodynamic support for the notion, but it persisted until the late 19th century, when experimentation in hull shape began with William Froude's theories and David W. Taylor's model experiments. Admiral David W. Taylor, Naval Constructor for the Navy at the turn of the century, was the first to introduce ship-model towing-tank research in naval ship design. He was responsible for the Navy Towing Tank at the Washington Navy Yard. This facility was replaced by the present large hydrodynamic laboratory in Maryland which bears Taylor's name. His early experiments resulted in such works as *Taylor's Standard Series* and other basic references still used today.

I have not yet mentioned the sail plan. The reason is, of course, that the ship designers of the time did not generally concern themselves with drawing the sail plan; instead, the builders customarily consulted the standard listings of spar dimensions for a particular size and rating of ship. This practice continued through the mid-19th century, until auxiliary steam engines gradually became the primary power on a vessel, and the sailing rig slowly shrank to insignificance.

Constitution's lofty sail plan, similar to that of her sister frigates, was unmistakable to her adversaries—even "hull down" on the horizon—as an identifying and unique rig; by contrast, ships of Nelson's navy and those of France seldom showed sails above the topgallant and rarely more than the main royal. Their spar dimensions were determined by the rigid limitations of the standard tables for spar size. The maximum sail plan as specified in the 1794 edition of *Steel's Elements of Mastmaking, Sailmaking, and Rigging* indicates a sail plan for frigates with royals on all three masts, double spritsails below the bowsprit, and studding sails (stun'sails) up through the topgallant on the fore and mainmasts as well as a driver (mizzen) extended by gaff and boom additions. There are also the staysails and jibs, with the highest staysails between the fore and mainmasts from the main topgallant mast stay (see Figure 1-10).

In contemporary artists' drawings and prints, the American *Constitution*-class frigate shows sail plans with a taller rig. The masts of *Constitution* and her sisters were allowed to reach a new proportionate height by extending the length of their poles above the topmast's upper crosstrees; this can be seen in the lithograph of *Constitution* vs. *Java*, drawn "under the direction of a witness to the action." See Figure 2-20 in Chapter Two illustrating this battle action in the War of 1812. Above their topmasts, there were two upper poles—topgallant mast and royal pole—and above the royal sail on all three masts was an extended length for another and uppermost sail, the newly adopted *skysail*.[2]

It was not until a half century later that any square-rigged ship dared set more sail on three masts. On the larger Yankee Clippers, some audacious captains finally topped the skysails with a triangular cloth called a moonraker. Very few ever carried such lofty sails in their regular sail plan. But one clipper ship built in Baltimore in 1851 and named *Seaman's Bride* had long enough upper poles above her royals and skysails to carry rectangular moon sails on all three masts. She was not an exceptionally large clipper ship, but she probably was the most extreme in proportionate sail-carrying ability, measured by the sail area/displacement ratio. This ratio's equation is used in comparing modern racing sailing yachts and usually computes to be near 20. The clipper ship *Seaman's Bride* computes out at 77. Her sail area was 63,000 square feet, and her displacement was 668 tons. The sail area/displacement ratio of *Constitution* is not readily available because we can only estimate her full sail area, but the ratio would probably be in the vicinity of 40.

On warships as well as on fast privateers and the later clipper ships, the upper sails and outer sails (stun'sails) were customarily considered expendable. They were taken in, of course, at the approach of heavy weather and were not carried into battle because of their vulnerability and awkwardness under conditions requiring maneuverability. Skysails soon became more than a novelty and were generally set flying—that is, with only a halyard to their small yard and without braces. These sails on *Constitution* were essentially cruising sails to enhance her passagemaking speeds. She used them regularly also to outrun enemy ships in a chase.

The new navy, and the world in 1800

The United States faced a hostile and belligerent world in 1800. Treaties were being made and broken with the Barbary states amid piratical terrorism. The upheavals in Europe, with Napoleon coming to power and the British response, were producing French privateers that plundered American shipping in the Caribbean and that eventually operated off the American coast. The naval establishment had been created by Congress in 1794. For the next few years, however, there was a reluctance on the part of Congress to authorize the construction of warships to deal with this growing problem. The eastern states were all for sending a naval force against the Barbary pirates. Those from the agricultural states to the west were just as content to go on paying "tribute," a euphemism for blackmail. By 1800, however, someone

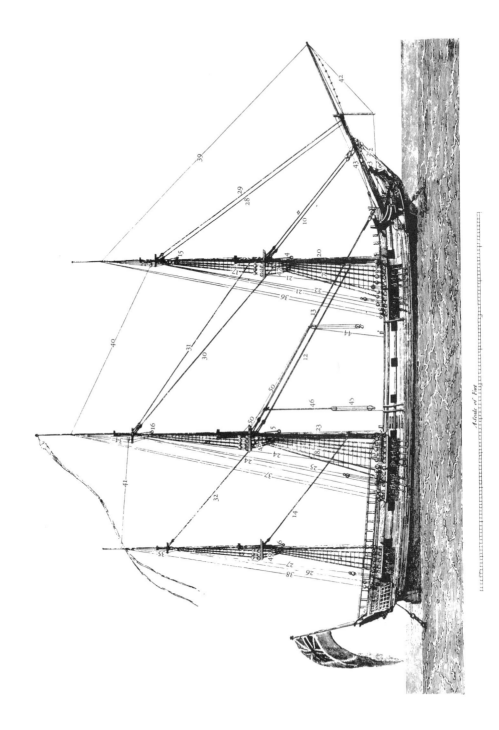

A Scale of Feet

Figure 1-8.

EXPLANATION OF THE REFERENCES ON THE PLATE DELINEATING THE STANDING RIGGING OF A SHIP

1. Gammoning
2. Bobstays
3. Bowsprit shrouds
4. Fore tackle pendants
5. Main tackle pendants
6. Mizzen burton pendants
7. Fore shrouds
8. Main shrouds
9. Mizzen shrouds
10. Fore preventer stay
11. Fore stay
12. Main preventer stay
13. Main stay
14. Mizzen stay
15. Fore topmast burton pendants
16. Main topmast burton pendants
17. Fore topmast shrouds
18. Main topmast shrouds
19. Mizzen topmast shrouds
20. Fore topmast breast backstay
21. Fore topmast standing backstay
22. Fore topmast shifting backstay
23. Main topmast breast backstay
24. Main topmast standing backstay
25. Main topmast shifting backstay
26. Mizzen topmast standing backstay
27. Mizzen topmast shifting backstay
28. Fore topmast preventer backstay
29. Fore topmast stay
30. Main topmast preventer stay
31. Main topmast stay
32. Mizzen topmast stay
33. Fore topgallant shrouds
34. Main topgallant shrouds
35. Mizzen topgallant shrouds
36. Fore topgallant standing backstays
37. Main topgallant standing backstays
38. Mizzen topgallant standing backstay
39. Fore topgallant stay
40. Main topgallant stay
41. Mizzen topgallant stay
42. Martingale stay
43. Bowsprit horse
44. Fore stay tackle
45. Main stay tackle
46. Main stay tackle pendant
47. Fore futtock shrouds
48. Main futtock shrouds
49. Mizzen futtock shrouds
50. Stay tackle tricing lines

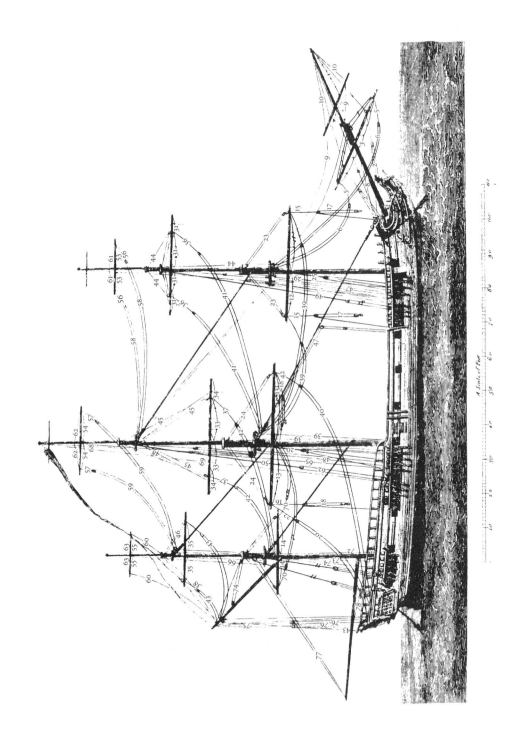

Figure 1-9.

EXPLANATION OF THE REFERENCES ON THE PLATE DELINEATING THE RUNNING RIGGING OF A SHIP

1. Jib horses
2. Jib guy pendants
3. Spritsail yard horses and stirrups
4. Spritsail topsail yard horses
5. Spritsail brace pendants
6. Spritsail braces
7. Spritsail lifts
8. Spritsail halyards
9. Spritsail topsail braces
10. Spritsail topsail lifts
11. Spritsail topsail halyards
12. Fore yard horses and stirrups
13. Main yard horses and stirrups
14. Cross jack horses
15. Fore yard tackle pendants
16. Main yard tackle pendants
17. Fore yard tackles
18. Main yard tackle pendants
19. Inner tricing line to the main yard tackle
20. Outer tricing line to the main yard tackle
21. Fore brace pendants
22. Main brace pendants
23. Fore lifts
24. Main lifts
25. Tye of the fore jeers
26. Tye of the main jeers
27. Fall of the fore jeers
28. Fall of the main jeers
29. Nave line of the fore truss pendants
30. Nave line of the main truss pendants
31. Fore topsail yard horses and stirrups
32. Fore topsail yard flemish horses
33. Main topsail yard horses and stirrups
34. Main topsail yard flemish horses
35. Mizzen topsail horses
36. Fore topsail brace pendants
37. Main topsail brace pendants
38. Mizzen topsail brace pendants
39. Fore braces
40. Main braces
41. Fore topsail braces
42. Main topsail braces
43. Mizzen topsail braces
44. Fore topsail lifts
45. Main topsail lifts
46. Mizzen topsail lifts
47. Fore topsail reef tackle pendants
48. Main topsail reef tackle pendants
49. Fore topsail tye
50. Main topsail tye
51. Fore topsail halyards
52. Main topsail halyards
53. Fore topgallant yard horses
54. Main topgallant yard horses
55. Mizzen topgallant yard horses
56. Fore topgallant brace pendants
57. Main topgallant brace pendants
58. Fore topgallant braces
59. Main topgallant braces
60. Mizzen topgallant braces
61. Fore topgallant lifts
62. Main topgallant lifts
63. Mizzen topgallant lifts
64. Fore topgallant halyards
65. Main topgallant halyards
66. Mizzen topgallant halyards
67. Fore royal halyard
68. Main royal halyard
69. Pendant halyard
70. Cross jack brace pendants
71. Cross jack braces
72. Cross jack lifts
73. Gaff throat halyards
74. Gaff peak halyards
75. Vang pendants
76. Vang falls
77. Boom topping lift
78. Guy pendant and tackle

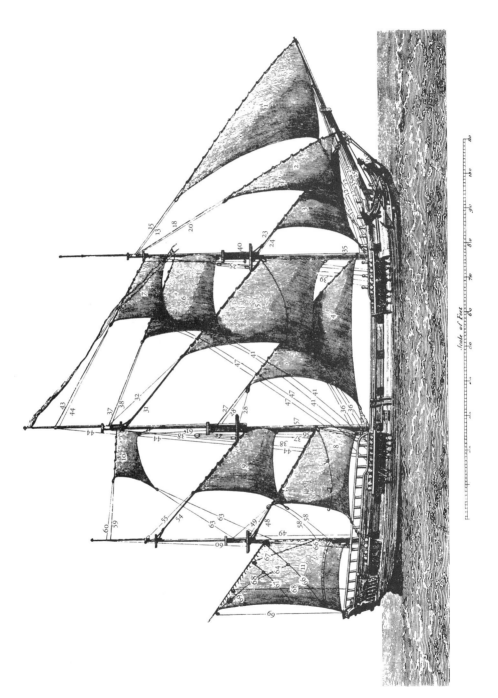

Figure 1-10.

EXPLANATION OF THE REFERENCES OF THE PLATE DELINEATING THE FORE-AND-AFT SAILS OF A SHIP

1. Jib
2. Fore topmast staysail
3. Fore staysail
4. Main staysail
5. Main topmast staysail
6. Middle staysail
7. Main topgallant staysail
8. Mizzen staysail
9. Mizzen topmast staysail
10. Mizzen topgallant staysail
11. Mizzen
12. Jib downhauler
13. Jib halyards
14. Jib sheets
15. Jib stay
16. Jib outhauler
17. Jib inhauler
18. Fore topmast stay
19. Fore topmast staysail downhauler
20. Fore topmast staysail halyards
21. Fore topmast staysail sheets
22. Fore topmast staysail outhauler
23. Fore preventer stay
24. Fore staysail halyards
25. Fore staysail downhauler
26. Fore staysail sheets
27. Main staysail stay
28. Main staysail halyards
29. Main staysail downhauler
30. Main staysail sheets
31. Main topmast preventer stay
32. Main topmast staysail halyards
33. Main topmast staysail downhauler
34. Main topmast staysail brails
35. Main topmast staysail tacks
36. Main topmast staysail sheets
37. Middle staysail stay
38. Middle staysail halyards
39. Middle staysail downhauler
40. Middle staysail tacks
41. Middle staysail sheets
42. Middle staysail tricing line
43. Main topgallant staysail stay
44. Main topgallant staysail halyards
45. Main topgallant staysail downhauler
46. Main topgallant staysail tacks
47. Main topgallant staysail sheets
48. Mizzen stay
49. Mizzen staysail halyards
50. Mizzen staysail downhauler
51. Mizzen staysail brails
52. Mizzen staysail tacks
53. Mizzen staysail sheets
54. Mizzen topmast stay
55. Mizzen topmast staysail halyards
56. Mizzen topmast staysail downhauler
57. Mizzen topmast staysail tacks
58. Mizzen topmast staysail sheets
59. Mizzen topgallant stay
60. Mizzen topgallant staysail halyards
61. Mizzen topgallant staysail downhauler
62. Mizzen topgallant staysail tacks
63. Mizzen topgallant staysail sheets
64. Tack of the mizzen course
65. Sheet of the mizzen course
66. Throat brails of the mizzen course
67. Middle brails of the mizzen course
68. Peak brails of the mizzen course
69. Fancy line

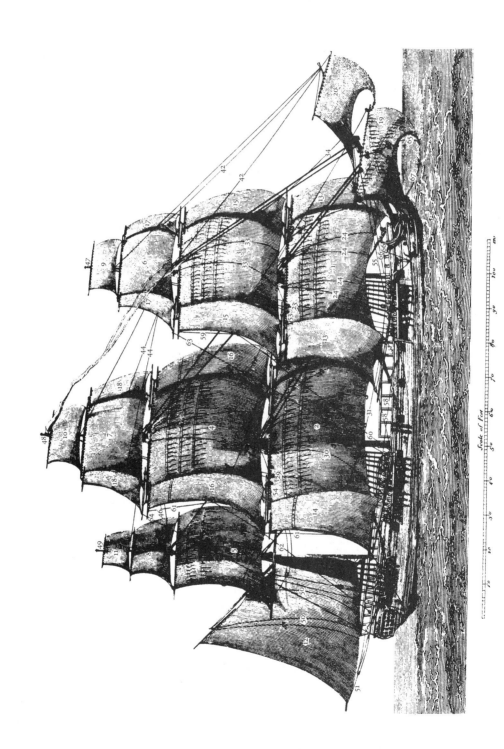

Figure 1-11.

EXPLANATION OF THE REFERENCES ON THE PLATE DELINEATING THE SQUARE SAILS OF A SHIP

1. Fore course
2. Main course
3. Fore topsail
4. Main topsail
5. Mizzen topsail
6. Fore topgallant sail
7. Main topgallant sail
8. Mizzen topgallant sail
9. Fore royal
10. Main royal
11. Mizzen royal
12. Driver
13. Fore studding sails
14. Main studding sails
15. Fore topmast studding sails
16. Main topmast studding sails
17. Fore topgallant studding sails
18. Main topgallant studding sails
19. Spritsail course
20. Spritsail topsail
21. Fore sail sheets
22. Fore sail tacks
23. Fore sail leech lines
24. Fore sail buntlines
25. Fore sail bowlines
26. Fore sail bowline bridles
27. Main sheets
28. Main tack
29. Main sail leech lines
30. Main sail buntlines
31. Main sail bowlines
32. Main sail bowline bridles
33. Fore topsail buntlines
34. Fore topsail bowlines
35. Fore topsail bowline bridles
36. Main topsail buntlines
37. Main topsail bowlines
38. Main topsail bowline bridles
39. Mizzen topsail buntlines
40. Mizzen topsail bowline
41. Mizzen topsail bowline bridles
42. Fore topgallant bowlines
43. Fore topgallant bowline bridles
44. Main topgallant bowlines
45. Main topgallant bowline bridles
46. Mizzen topgallant bowline
47. Fore royal halyards
48. Main royal halyards
49. Mizzen royal halyards
50. Driver halyards
51. Driver sheet
52. Driver downhauler
53. Fore studding sail inner halyards
54. Main studding sail inner halyards
55. Fore studding sail boom guy
56. Fore studding sail tacks
57. Fore studding sail sheet
58. Main studding sail tacks
59. Fore topmast studding sail downhauler
60. Fore topmast studding sail tack
61. Main topmast studding sail downhauler
62. Main topmast studding sail tack
63. Fore topgallant studding sail tack
64. Main topgallant studding sail tack
65. Spritsail clew line
66. Spritsail buntline
67. Spritsail sheets
68. Spritsail topsail sheets

must have finally remembered the ringing words of John Harper a few years earlier, "Millions for defense, but not one cent for tribute."

Several acts of Congress had authorized 12 ships of not less than 32 guns each, 12 ships of not less than 20 guns each, and six of no less than 18 guns, plus several galleys and revenue cutters. It should be noted, however, that while this was the authorized navy of U.S. warships, for lack of funding not all of these ships were built.

The immediate and most threatening enemy was, of all nations, this country's earliest and most reliable friend—the emerging Republic of France. France had just struggled from beneath the anarchistic and bloody revolution to be taken over by the militaristic rule of Napoleon Bonaparte, who saw the world as an unlimited target of conquest. This early naval activity between the United States and France has become known as the Quasi War, because while war was never officially declared, the encounters—many of them in American harbors—were full of hostility.

Major U.S. Navy warships

The following is a brief list of the vessels of our early Navy in the first decade of the 19th century, with notes on each ship's final destiny.

U.S. Frigates	CONSTITUTION CLASS	Launched	Disposition
Constitution	44 guns	1797	Survivor, still in commission 1993
President	44 guns	1800	Captured by British Squadron January 14, 1815. Broken up Portsmouth, England, 1817
United States	44 guns	1797	Lost to Confederates April 10, 1861. Broken up 1865, Norfolk, VA

U.S. Frigates	CONSTELLATION CLASS	Launched	Disposition
Constellation	36 guns	1797	Broken up 1853, Norfolk, VA
Congress	36 guns	1799	Broken up 1836, Norfolk, VA
Chesapeake	36 guns	1799	Captured by British HMS *Shannon* July 13, 1813. Broken up 1820

U.S. Subscription Frigates

Philadelphia	36 guns	1799	Captured by Tripolitan pirates, destroyed by *Constitution* boarding party, February 1803
New York	36 guns	1800	Burned in Washington Navy Yard by British, August 1814
Essex	32 guns	1799	Lost in combat 1814 in South Pacific to British frigate and corvette
Boston	28 guns	1799	Burned in Washington Navy Yard by British, August 1814
Adams	28 guns	1799	Burned in Penobscot Bay to prevent capture, September 1814
John Adams	28 guns	1799	Broken up Norfolk Navy Yard, 1829

Captured Frigates Taken into U.S. Navy

Macedonian (British)	40 guns		Captured 1812 by frigate *United States*. Broken up Norfolk Navy Yard, 1836
Alert (British ship, sloop-of-war)	20 guns		Captured 1812 by frigate *Essex*. Broken up Norfolk Navy Yard, 1829

Constructing *Constitution*

The contract for building one of the Navy's large 44-gun frigates was given to the Hartt Brothers Shipyard in Boston in 1795. In that same year, Edmund Hartt, the director of the yard and a master shipbuilder, and the naval constructor, George Claighorne, proceeded with the construction of this new frigate, ultimately to be named *Constitution*. (An agreement on names of each new frigate came in the following year).

There was nothing particularly unusual about the way the Hartt Brothers put together *Constitution* (details on the frigate's construction are in Chapter Four). Essentially they followed the drawings and construction process originated by Joshua Humphreys and his draftsman William Doughty. At the time, a ship's design consisted essentially of the hull's configuration in three projections—the sheer profile, the half-breadth plan, and the body plan. These are apparent in the Doughty's illustration in Figure 1-3.

There were no detailed drawings for the ship's structure or even general structural drawings. There were, however, written instructions for the scantlings (timber and planking dimensions) and for any special structures or departures from conventional shipbuilding practices. These instructions can be considered today as a form of specifications.

The only mystery surrounding *Constitution*'s construction is whether or not the builders put diagonal rider frames in the ships's bottom on top of the ceiling—as specified by Humphreys. Diagonal rider frames—designed to prevent "hogging," or the upward curvature of the hull at midkeel—were not standard or common design elements in a frigate's structure. On the other hand, the 44-gun vessels were built to a newer concept. These frigates were large and heavy, very close in hull dimension but slightly smaller than the popular 74-gun ships. And the 74-gun ships were built with diagonal rider frames. But now, nearly 200 years after *Constitution* was built, there is no evidence of diagonal rider frames. They are not now in the ship and there is no evidence that they ever were. Some say these rider frames were removed during an extensive overhaul in the mid-19th century. Indeed, there were several such overhauls, but there is no record or maintenance log that indicates such a major de-structuring. To the contrary, records reporting an early evidence of ship hogging indicate that these longitudinal strength timbers were not a part of the ship's original structure.

At any rate, the construction of *Constitution* proceeded full course without any notable departure from the usual methodology: laying the keel, framing the ship, placing the keelson, and construction of the ceiling, external planking, and decking, and finally, finishing the exterior. There were a few delays caused by Washington's on-again off-again treaties with the Mediterranean pirate countries, but by the end of October 1797, she was ready for launching.

Launching problems

Constitution still had not been fitted out when the first American warships put to sea in September 1797—first *Ganges*, a converted merchant ship of 24 guns, under Captain Dale, followed by *Constellation*, 36 guns, under Captain Truxton—heading for the Caribbean to square off against the French ships in the Quasi War.

At this time, *Constitution* was a month away from launching. A common rumor among shipbuilders was that if a ship had bad luck in launching, she would always be plagued by bad luck. This may have been true or not: One of *Constitution*'s sister frigates, *United States*, was badly damaged in launching, and she carried the scars throughout her career, which was not altogether distinguished. *Constitution* was not damaged, but became embarrassingly stuck on the launching ways; it took three attempts before she finally became waterborne.

To the shipbuilder, this sort of performance, rightly or wrongly, reflected badly upon his credibility. And while it is true that such things should not happen, as ships became larger throughout the last century it became obvious that the launching procedure was fraught with hazards—and that there was more at risk in costs and in danger to lives and property. In modern times, perhaps since the late 19th century, the naval architect, the ship's designer, has been responsible for a safe launching.

Sending a massive body weighing hundreds, even a thousand or more tons down an incline requires serious engineering preparation. If done wrong, sometimes the ship moves too fast, and the arresting system is inadequate to stop it within a safe distance. Sometimes the ship comes to a stop partway down the launching ways—too far from floating! Sometimes it may slew sideways and fall from the launching ways. And, in recent times as well as historically, upon reaching the water a ship may fail to float upright—capsizing! Such catastrophes are rare, and there is little or no excuse for them. The only excuse at the time of *Constitution*'s launching two centuries ago was that there was little beyond experience and empirical knowledge to safeguard against such mistakes.

Today, launching is even more of a major engineering undertaking, but evolution in procedural guidance and science now ensure reasonable safety. The problem in Boston in October 1797, when *Constitution* stubbornly came to rest partway down the launching ways, was blamed on the insufficient downward angle, or *declivity*, of the ways.

At the time of *Constitution*'s launching, the launching process had remained virtually unchanged since the 16th century. And with minor variations, it was a universal accepted practice. It works like this: The ship is most commonly supported in the building process by keel blocks and side shoring, both of which rest firmly on the shipyard's solid ground or reinforced ground base which slopes toward the water. As launching day approaches, the ways—two broad wooden (or steel) track-like paths—are prepared on both sides of the keel blocks at equal and adequate positions, and lubricant is spread upon them. A launching cradle is built on top of the ground ways, consisting of blocking to fit the ship's bilges for about two-thirds or more of its length.

Within a short time before launching (a day or so), the keel blocks and structure that has supported the growing ship are removed, and the ship settles into the launching cradle. On launching day, the only thing preventing the ship from beginning the fateful journey to the water is a heavy trigger-blocking mechanism locking the launching cradle in place. In the day of the federal frigates, the custom was to block the movement of the launching cradle by angling one or two heavy timbers against it below the end of the ship. Beneath this critical structure was a pit large enough for a man to jump into after he had struck the final blow with a sledgehammer, knocking out the trigger blocks holding the ship. This hazardous job was sometimes given to a brave volunteer or to a convict promised freedom.

No one knows why *Constitution* halted or faltered in her journey to the water, but there could have been a number of reasons other than lack of adequate declivity.

The three 44-gun frigates were the largest ships in the experience of American shipbuilders in 1796–97. They were not only heavier, they were substantially longer. The launching formulae used for smaller vessels were apparently not totally reliable for these heavy frigates.

As was told earlier, *Constitution*'s sister, *United States* encountered serious damage in launching. This may have been the result of inadequate lubricant—the heat of friction in launching is a function of the force or weight on the moving surface. (Launching is generally accompanied by smoking ways from the generated heat.) The greater the weight, the more heat to consume the lubricant. Temperature and humidity can also affect the launching ways. These factors may well have not been adequate for the heavier frigates. None of the lighter three frigates encountered launching trouble. It would seem more probable that one or more of the various controlling factors other than declivity held up *Constitution*'s flotation.

In any event, *Constitution* finally was afloat by October 1797. At this time, however, Congress was satisfied at least momentarily with the "peace" arrangements with the Barbary terrorists. No more frigates could be supported, and she was put in limbo—until 1798 brought new threats to our shipping. In March of that year, *Constitution* under Congressional authorization began fitting out for sea. The Quasi War with France, particularly in the Caribbean and the southern coastal states, was becoming very troublesome. There were many American merchant ships being plundered and captured by French cruisers and privateers. Some 32 ships, brigs, and schooners were reported lost by the Secretary of State to the President, and ten times as many were reported in the newspaper.

It was time that *Constitution* got to sea.

Constitution's Early Career

At summer's end in 1798, *Constitution* was completed. Her commanding officer, Captain Samuel Nicholson, mustered his new crew, read his orders, hoisted his pennant, and, with little ceremony, ordered the ship underway for her first voyage. It was a low-key commissioning for an untried warship; none present that day could foresee the long and eventful career of this great ship.

And she was, even at the beginning of her career, a great ship. *Constitution* was the largest American warship yet to put to sea; indeed, she was the largest frigate in any navy. Even before her first naval engagement, she was recognized as a powerful machine of destruction.

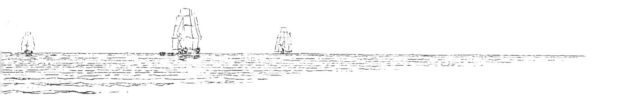

Shakedown cruise

Constitution's first voyage was to the West Indies, where French warships under their adventurous new revolutionary government were harassing foreign ships—especially American ships. Her smaller sister *Constellation* had been in these waters for a year or more and had successfully taken the French frigate *Insurgente*. In her own encounters with the smaller French privateers, *Constitution* wasn't as successful. Although at 13.5 knots she was fast for a frigate, her size and weight, as well as her complex rig, hampered her maneuverability. In company with similar ships, her performance was encouraging. In a matched sailing contest, she substantially outperformed the British frigate HMS *Santa Margareta*.

She also outgunned and captured a formidable Spanish fort, sustaining no damage or casualties herself. For the young frigate, these encounters laid the groundwork for her growing reputation, and for the growing international respect for the American Navy.

The turn of the new century brought political changes and new policies for the naval establishment, however, and *Constitution* was ordered home. From 1801 through most of 1803 she and the other new frigates were laid up without commission in New York—"in ordinary," as it was called, the result of policy changes in the new presidential administration. Thomas Jefferson's idealism, which had served the country so well before and during the American Revolution, failed him in the face of a hostile world order. Jefferson was fundamentally opposed to a strong naval establishment, and was inclined to turn his back on threats from abroad, whether from pirates in the Mediterranean, foreign privateering, or bullying by England. Jefferson's opposition to maintaining a strong navy, especially these larger, expensive ships, found a sympathetic ear in a Congress who saw the political value in opposing the expensive support of a naval force working in far-off oceans.

The Tripolitan wars

The Jeffersonian defense philosophy was political and simplistic: Put the great but expensive ships in storage. After all, American citizens were protected from foreign threats by the great oceans—watery barriers that took some four weeks or more to cross. The country was also beginning to look westward, and the political philosophy favored the frontier spirit of

Figure 2-1. This finely detailed image shows a truly native Barbary corsair of the late 18th and early 19th century—the type of pirate craft that terrorized our young country's merchant fleet. The artist, Jean Jerome Baugean, a French engraver and marine artist of the early 1800s, simply calls it a "Mediterranean Corsaire, entering the anchorage with a following wind." This three-masted lateen-rigged vessel is a Chebec. The three large lateen sails, the main here being furled, were sometimes replaced by square sails on the fore and main masts that were extended proportionately. Fast and maneuverable, these Chebecs carried large crews and were sometimes equipped with oars, ensuring mobility even in flat calms.

independence. As George Washington had warned before leaving office, America should make "no foreign entanglements." And so, as a result of easy political thinking, the American naval force became a "gunboat navy" in which vessels could be quickly provided when and where—and if—they were needed. This mentality culminated in attempts by the Secretary of the Navy to provide a small squadron of gunboats, each about 40 feet in length, with a single forward-mounted gun—weapons suited only for coastal defense.

But at the dawn of the 19th century, laying up the great frigates was not unlike a frontiersman surrounded by heavily armed savages feeling secure because he had an unloaded gun safely locked in the attic. America's defense problems lay farther afield than her immediate coastline, particularly in the Mediterranean, where Tripolitan pirates continued seizing

Figure 2-2. This painting shows a small pirate corsair taking a typical unarmed American merchant vessel in the Mediterranean. The rig of the pirate craft is not typical; it appears to be an eight-gun, cutter-rigged English naval type—a smaller but faster, more maneuverable vessel than the larger, square-rigged merchant ship from Boston. The Barbary pirates frequently used captured vessels of European origin.

Figure 2-3. An excellent ship portrait by Jean Jerome Baugean, who before the French Revolution was designated "Engraver to the King." Baugean was fascinated by ships and boats of every size and type, and his skill has provided here and on following pages accurate line drawings of watercraft of his time. This is his view of the most impressive type of sailing warship under sail, a first-rate ship-of-the-line, with more than 100 guns. It is not identified, except that she is obviously British, as he indicates— "of three decks under all sail." She is accompanied by a 12-gun naval cutter.

American ships and holding American seamen hostage. To settle its conscience and mollify the increasingly strident complaints of those merchants who still attempted to maintain crucial foreign trade, Congress, in February 1802, recognized that a state of war existed with Tripoli, and authorized the Navy "to attack and seize Tripolitan shipping." It's unlikely that this threat caused the Bey of Tripoli to lose much sleep, or to restrain his ever-increasing acts of piracy on defenseless American ships. After all, at that time the United States had but one vessel of war on active duty.

To provide a modest display of armed defense against the Tripolitans,

Baugean del. et sculp

Vaisseau de ligne en calme, se faisant remorquer.

Figure 2-4. A 74-gun ship-of-the-line, a third-rate vessel with two gun decks, carried heavier guns than a large frigate such as *Constitution*; approximately 50 percent more firepower, the combined weight of the broadside guns. They were popular in both the French and British navies, and the United States began to build several of them late in the War of 1812 and following years; they were not commissioned until well after the war, however, and became useless floating fortresses.

and to support the Congressional declaration of war, the Navy was finally ordered in May 1801 to maintain two frigates on station in the Mediterranean. These frigates, however, were ineffective. Tripolitan pirate vessels simply went about their business and avoided American warships. For their part, the American ships steered clear of any confrontation. Doubtless it was pleasant cruising for the Americans, with their ships alternating between station and shore visits in Italy and France. This situation continued until the time when it became clear the U.S. Navy had to act.

From 1796 to 1798, there had been a succession of so-called peace treaties between the United States and Tripoli, which amounted to nothing more than tribute agreements. But even these were violated, and as tenuous peace with the Barbary states crumbled, it became obvious that a more serious show of force was necessary to stop the piracy. Commodore Edward Preble was ordered to fit out *Constitution* as the flagship of a third squadron to strengthen the Mediterranean fleet, but he and his squadron had barely arrived when the Navy suffered a loss it could ill afford. In October 1803, the U.S. frigate *Philadelphia*, already on station, ran aground on a reef near the entrance to Tripoli harbor while chasing blockade-running pirates. Helpless, she was captured by Tripolitans and her officers and crew taken hostage. Preble and his new squadron faced an immediate crisis, but as we shall see, the powerful new force and its resourceful officers were equal to the task.

Constitution and her contemporaries in the Mediterranean

Preble had sailed from Boston in August 1803. The squadron vessels were: *Nautilus*, 12 guns; *Vixen*, 12 guns; *Siren*, 16 guns; *Enterprise*, 12 guns; and *Argus*, 16 guns. Also part of the command, already on station, was the ill-fated frigate *Philadelphia*, 36 guns.

Enterprise, the third U.S. Navy war vessel of that name, was built on the Eastern Shore of Maryland in 1799, and was described on her builder's certificate as a "sharp-built" fast schooner, privateer type—a prototype of the schooners soon to become famous in the War of 1812 as privateers, the Baltimore Clippers. These topsail schooners were built in abundance in the upper Chesapeake Bay region and fanned out on the oceans to prey heavily on British merchant shipping during the 1812 conflict, carrying the war into England's home waters. Built by Henry Spencer near St. Michaels, Maryland, *Enterprise* was approximately 85 feet length on deck, 60 feet length of keel, 23 feet beam, and 135 measured tons. As originally

Figure 2-5. This painting shows the Navy schooner USS *Enterprise* taking a large, armed Barbary terrorist vessel from Tripoli, Libya, in 1801. Enterprise was later in *Constitution*'s squadron when she arrived in 1803.

fitted out, she carried 12 long six-pounders and was so rated when taken into the Navy.

Nautilus and *Vixen* were both sharp-built schooners, built in 1803 by William Price of Fells Point, Baltimore, later a builder of successful Baltimore Clipper privateers. USS *Argus* and *Siren* (*Syren*) were both 16-gun brigs built in Boston and Philadelphia, respectively, in 1803.

Commodore Preble had under his command a fine squadron of new and relatively new vessels commanded by equally new young officers: Lieutenant John Smith in *Vixen*; Lieutenant Richard Somers in *Nautilus*; Lieutenant Charles Stewart in *Siren*; Lieutenant Stephen Decatur, Jr., in *Argus*; and Lieutenant Isaac Hull commanding *Enterprise*. The latter two vessels and their commanding officers were to exchange places to adjust their relative seniority, in that *Enterprise* was already on station in the Mediterranean and *Argus* was rated above *Enterprise* as a war vessel for reasons of dimension. Most of these young men, whom Preble derisively char-

Baugean del. et sculp.

Figure 2-6. This Baugean engraving shows an American frigate, a fifth rate according to the British system, underway into an anchorage. Although the artist does not identify the ship, it is believed to be *Constitution*, for she was in the Mediterranean during the years Baugean was illustrating warships there. The frigate is a 44, and there were only two others, *United States* and *President*. According to the *Constitution*'s appearance here, it was a time after *President*'s departure and before the *United States* took up station in the Mediterranean. Baugean's rendering shows a bowsprit/jibboom assembly that is shorter than it should be according to *Constitution*'s original hull profile. *Constitution*'s collision with *President* in 1804 definitely shortened her bowsprit; likely this is a temporary jibboom assembly waiting for a full restoration in a better time and place. It is more difficult to explain the figurehead, which *Constitution* lost in the same accident; on the other hand, Baugean has been unreliable in detailing figureheads.

Figure 2-7. Baugean clearly identifies this frigate as "*le President*," and she undoubtedly is. According to the artist, she is sailing in rising wind under reefed topsails. It is a reasonable guess that *Constitution* had much the same quartering view.

acterized early on as being "but schoolboys," are now names carved in granite on buildings and monuments in our nation's capital, at the U.S. Naval Academy in Annapolis, and elsewhere in our annals of history—young men truly sailing to glory under crusty Edward Preble, a veteran of the Continental Navy of the Revolution.

In September 1803, when *Constitution* arrived in the Mediterranean, she was also young and in her prime—as yet untried in combat with enemy warships, but well shaken down in her West Indies cruise of 1798–1800. She had now been taken over by an older, well-seasoned naval officer and fitted out according to his wishes. This fitting out and adaptation, as we shall see, was a matter of naval tradition. A commanding officer could

Figure 2-8. Another frigate as Baugean saw it—again not identified, but clearly one of the American original six, one of the three 36-gun ships of the *Constellation*-class. The artist observes that the crew is "drying their hammocks." It was probably Thursday, traditional hammock-scrubbing day.

change his ship's character according to his own ideas; he was not restrained by bureaucratic orders or the basic plans of naval constructors. Such localized freedom to alter or change had existed from the beginnings of the Navy in the American Revolution—a concept, in fact, carried over from the British naval tradition. It was not until after the first decade of the 19th century that the Secretary of the Navy authorized the creation of a committee for departmental operation, which provided a strong bureaucratic establishment ashore that gradually took over the technology of naval ships and warfare.

In any case, there is evidence that *Constitution* first began to change from her original design and image under the direction of Edward Preble. Now squadron commodore, Preble was the first of several rigorous commanders assigned to *Constitution*. He ran a "taut" ship, and his sour demeanor was not eased by his troublesome stomach ulcers. The changes that took place on *Constitution* in fitting out for this voyage were not drastic. Preble, in anticipating the sort of hostility he would likely be engaged in, basically added more guns and carronades.

I cannot help but reflect on my own experiences in a later, somewhat similar situation; this may help us measure the march of marine technology throughout this account and the remainder of the frigate's long life—a life nearly as long as our country's. In 1936 I was a young officer on board another Navy flagship fitting out for Mediterranean duty. The light cruiser USS *Raleigh* was detached from the Pacific fleet and ordered into the old Gosport Navy Yard in Norfolk, Virginia, to be refitted for service as the flagship of a renewed Mediterranean squadron, which had been abandoned in the late 1920s as a result of the international agreements on naval ship reductions—a disarmament treaty meant to reduce the chance of war. But presidential administrations change, economics change, and international politics in the 1930s were volatile, with a new and strident tune in Europe orchestrated by Benito Mussolini, Adolf Hitler, and Francisco Franco. President Franklin D. Roosevelt decided that we again needed a naval squadron in Mediterranean waters.

The *Raleigh* was not equipped for such independent self-sufficiency, and needed extensive modification to become the mothership for a squadron of four destroyers and a Coast Guard cutter. Consequently, among other changes that occurred in those nine summer weeks, we had installed an enlarged sick bay with surgical and dental facilities, a reinforced anti-aircraft battery, better movie projectors, enlarged quarters for the flag officers' staff as well as the squadron's commander, and berthing facilities for a ship's band and honor guard. One other change that I know must have taken place was enlarged refrigeration storage—I remember that at the end of two years on station we were still using frozen food that had been put aboard in Norfolk in August 1936.

There are no line-item comparisons with *Constitution*'s fitting-out for the Mediterranean, but the overall planning has some similarities—and

Figure 2-9. A brig-of-war, a smaller vessel with substantial gunpower—20 guns, probably 9-pounders on the gun deck. This ship is probably American or British. There were several brigs-of-war under Preble's command in the Mediterranean.

some contrasts. Our ship, *Raleigh*, was a cruiser—a post-World War I type that was in the 1930s comparable to a frigate of 1800 (*Raleigh* even had six broadside guns). Both were capable of single-ship duty with seagoing endurance, self-sufficiency, and hard-hitting firepower. *Raleigh*'s complement was very similar to *Constitution*'s: 550 men and 30 officers. She too was a ship of relatively high cruising speed and maneuverability. When we departed from Norfolk in late September in the wake of a hurricane, I was acting navigator; the captain ordered a great-circle course from the Chesapeake Lightship to Cape Saint Vincent, Portugal, at a sustained speed of 20 knots. No satellite navigation, no star sights, and only one or

Figure 2-10. This engraving shows a schooner-brig—sometimes called a brigantine, but the term would be incorrect this early in the 19th century. Close examination of the rig reveals that the main or after mast is that of a typical schooner, but with two parts, the long section supporting the large gaff mainsail and the topmast. In this vessel both topmasts are rigged with poles for topgallants and fore royal. This is an American warship pierced for 22 guns.

two sun sights—the navigation was nearly all an exercise in dead reckoning. We raised Cape Saint Vincent Light early on the eighth day and rendezvoused with USS *Quincy*, a new light cruiser that had temporarily kept the station until our arrival.

Constitution arrived on September 12, 1803, and rendezvoused in Gibraltar with the U.S. frigate *Philadelphia*, 36 guns, under Captain William Bainbridge, who gave Commodore Preble the welcome news of his recent capture of a Moroccan pirate in possession of an American

Figure 2-11. An American double-topsail schooner of 20 guns, anchored near a brig-of-war of approximately the same size. It is rather difficult in this period to differentiate between schooner and brig. The definitive difference is in the length of the lower masts: Those of a schooner are always considerably longer to hoist a larger gaff-rigged sail. Also, the schooner had the advantage of large fore-and-aft sails dominating the squaresails, making her more closewinded than a brig. This factor was becoming more recognized and appreciated in the early 19th century. Note the number and quantity of large headsails. These vessels also were important in the American Mediterranean squadron.

ship—and a letter from the governor of Tangier, Morocco, authorizing capture of American vessels. Preble, realizing that Morocco had to be dealt with while the iron was still hot, so to speak, ordered Bainbridge to proceed on into the Mediterranean and reestablish the blockade of Tripoli; he then moved *Constitution* over to the shores of Tangier, taking with him a mighty display of naval strength which included the veteran and home-bound frigates *New York*, *Boston*, and *John Adams* as well as his accompanying third-squadron schooners and brigs. As he had hoped, the sudden appearance of this formidable naval force, with four frigates and an assortment of rakish-looking armed schooners and brigs, had an immediate effect on the Emperor of Morocco, who must have felt that the wrath of Allah had descended upon him for authorizing the capture of a humble American merchant brig named *Celia*. The Emperor hastily shifted responsibility in the *Celia* incident to the governor in Tangier, whom he immediately disposed of by ending his tenure as governor. He further tried to placate the American officers with gifts and negotiations. The issue was resolved by concluding or reestablishing a previous peace treaty without the provision of tribute. Preble's tour was beginning well, all because of the highly visible impact of naval power—a fact certainly not lost in the Washington halls of state diplomacy.

It must be acknowledged, then as well as now, that a powerful vessel of war—whether a gun-bristling frigate of the early 19th century or a long, low battleship of the 20th century—appearing at sunrise off a harbor entrance, makes an emphatic statement. *Constitution* by herself in the autumn of 1803 was such a ship, the largest and heaviest frigate the United States then deployed, newly fitted out and ready for duty, only four years from her original commissioning, with a fresh crew and a no-nonsense commodore. As technologically advanced in her day as an *Aegis*-class guided missile cruiser of today, *Constitution* alone would have made a thought-provoking display in 1803 before a recalcitrant group of Barbary terrorists. In fact, such a modern *Aegis* cruiser as the USS *Vicksburg*, with its multiple array of the latest weapons, has also made such a statement to the present-day nations of the Near East.

Let us build that image a bit more graphically, for this is probably the period in her long life that *Constitution* was looking her best. No detail nor profile drawings of the frigate survived from this period, but after considerable study I believe that my reconstructive drawing (Figure 2-12) is reasonably authentic. Her hull profile shown here puts her on her load waterline. She still shows but 15 gun ports on her gun deck level; a 16th (bridle) port was cut some years later under the command of Captain William

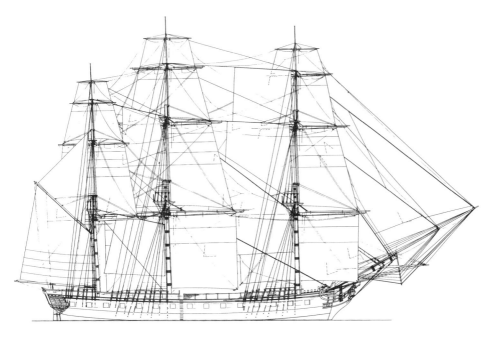

Figure 2-12. The outboard profile and sail plan of USS *Constitution* in the first years of the 19th century. She probably appeared very much as shown in this draft when she set out for the Mediterranean in 1803, with the goal of suppressing pirate activity and ending, as she did, the American humiliation of tribute and hostage capture and ransom—the same terrorist scenario of recent times.

Bainbridge. She displays her first and original figurehead, of which there is no graphic record—it has not been well shown in any contemporary paintings of her early career—and so my very small depiction of it here must be somewhat speculative. Measuring approximately 7 feet from heel to head, it has been authentically described as a figure of Hercules dressed in a lion's skin, brandishing a club—or, some say, a scroll representing the U.S. Constitution—and "standing upon the rock of Independence." It was carved by John Skillin, who was recommended by the renowned figure-head designer William Rush. This original figure later would be lost in *Constitution*'s unhappy collision with her sister frigate *President* in September 1804, when returning from a bombardment of Tripoli, described later in this chapter.

In the forward area, the ship still retained the original graceful curves of her cutwater bow head, and the graceful head knees and trailboards as her designer originally drew them. The bowsprit, too, is shown at its original steeve angle, not at the lower angle frequently shown in later reconstructed sail plans and profiles. At this early period, the philosophy of the bowsprit revolved around the continued use of the centuries-old spritsail forward, and the need to keep it clear of the sea at level, and braced up hard vertically. There is no justification for the depiction of a lower bowsprit angle on a ship at this point in history. Lower-angled bowsprits did begin to show up on Baltimore sharp-built schooners for the purpose of increasing the foretriangle area, but this low angle did not come into evidence on larger ships until much later.

Aft on the quarterdeck the bulwarks of the spar deck have been built in between the stanchions shown in the original design (see Figure 1-3). This is presumed to be part of the fitting-out ordered by Commodore Preble in preparing for Mediterranean service. Solid bulwarks topped by hammock nettings better protect the exposed gun crews on the spar deck from musket fire, flying splinters, and boarders. The spar deck along the ship's waist is still open, perhaps because there was no exposed activity in this area of the ship during battle. The guns that later brought the battery's total to more than 50 have not yet appeared on the spar deck forward, and *Constitution* still carries between 44 and 50 guns, with some variation among the number of carronades. She probably carried a long bow chaser forward, but it has not been drawn in this view. What is interesting here is not the frigate's battery of weapons, which waxed and waned, but the ship's overall profile and structure.

There is no change in the original design of quarter galleries, which rise so gracefully above the terminal upturn of the main wale aft.

The rigging and sail plan, which were subject to the greatest changes and whims of the various commanding officers, show here as a maximum spread of sail area—short of rigging the studding sails, the yards for which are housed on the appropriate yardarms. She shows an extremely large spanker with a gaff topsail, as well as a large spread of jibs and staysails in her foretriangle. In several contemporary drawings of *Constitution* from the very early 19th century, she shows small upper crosstrees on fore and main to give additional support to the long upper mast poles. This enormous spread of sail stemmed from the need to outrun large (74-gun) enemy vessels, and represented the proud spirit of some of her young captains, such as Hull, Stewart, Bainbridge, and others.

The sail profile reconstructed here is according to spar dimensions of the *Constitution* after she was refitted in Boston in 1803, and is in marked contrast to the contemporary engraving by Jean Jerome Baugean, Figure 2-6. While the ship in this finely detailed drawing is not identified by the artist, it is believed to be *Constitution* drawn prior to the War of 1812 when she was in the Mediterranean. The ship is easily recognized as one of the three heavy American frigates, showing the proper number of gunports and lofty masts. Her bowsprit/jibboom assembly seems to have been shortened, and this may reflect the result of her collision with USS *President* in 1804; this shortened jibboom may be evidence of an incomplete repair. However, she still exhibits her figurehead, which is said to have been lost in the unfortunate encounter. This drawing also shows a closed waist, which may also have been accomplished in one of the shipyards where she went for repairs—at Malta, Lisbon, or Syracuse.

After Preble's forced stand-down of the Emperor of Morocco at Tangier, he proceeded on to the middle Mediterranean, where he heard a rumor of the *Philadelphia* disaster from a British frigate he had spoken with a few days out of Malta; it was confirmed on his arrival at Malta, where letters from Captain Bainbridge awaited him. Preble immediately fell to planning a response to Tripoli, ordering *Constitution* to proceed on to the ancient port of Syracuse, in southern Sicily, where he established a base and a friendly relationship with the governor.

After studying the location and disposition of *Philadelphia*, Preble concluded that it would not be possible to save her, instead deciding on a daring plan to destroy her. Lieutenant Stephen Decatur, together with five

Figure 2-13. This shows USS *Enterprise*, a Navy schooner of some 16 guns, boarding a Tripolitan pirate—a typical close encounter resorting to face-to-face combat with edged weapons. The pirate vessel appears to have lost its foremast, while its bowsprit has penetrated the schooner's rigging. Fighting seems to be continuing, judging by the boarding axes in the hands of the American crew.

other officers, including one Midshipman McDonough and 62 volunteers, would carry out a detailed plan of destruction under cover of night: A captured Mediterranean trading vessel out of Tripoli, renamed *Intrepid*, would carry the armed boarding party into Tripoli's inner harbor and alongside *Philadelphia*, where they would recapture her from the Tripolitan crew on board, rig explosives, fire the ship, and be away before the heavy guns from the Tripolitan fort and fleet awoke—they hoped. Their backup ship would be the U.S. brig *Siren* under Lieutenant Charles Stewart.

This brilliant but complex night raid was carried out nearly flawlessly. An unexpected drop in the wind as they neared *Philadelphia* left the raiders momentarily at the mercy of the Tripolitan crew, whose lookout had just identified approaching attackers, but they managed to haul themselves by

Figure 2-14. Titled "Battle of Tripoli," this magnificent large oil painting by Michele F. Corne, painted in 1805, is perhaps unique. Talented artists contemporary with *Constitution*'s early career produced images of her in engraved drawings, watercolors, lithographs, and other media, but this is the only large painting and is a showpiece in the U.S. Naval Academy's collection of marine art. Unfortunately, in an oil painting, with its gradation of color and light and dark tones, the details are often lost. The painting reveals the high feelings of the moment and perhaps some of the precision in detail, but actual geometry suffers. It nevertheless reflects the great task of Commodore Preble in dealing with Libyan terrorists.

rope within boarding range and get aboard, where they fought a quick and valiant action. The Tripolitans surrendered after most had jumped overboard, and the American boarders departed the burning and exploding *Philadelphia*, rejoined their small *Intrepid*, and wafted out of the harbor to rejoin *Siren* amid heavy, frantic, but fortunately inaccurate gunfire from 100 or more cannons. The only damage to the ketch was a hole through the topsail.

Commodore Preble in *Constitution* immediately established a strict blockade of Tripoli, which he soon followed with a well-planned series of aggressive attacks. Having first arranged with the King of Sicily for the use of six gunboats and two bomb (heavy mortar)-carrying vessels, Preble together with his own squadron proceeded with the first bombardment of Tripoli.

Of this bombardment fleet, only *Constitution* and the bomb-carrying vessels could really be effective against the heavily walled and fortified city (see Figure 2-14). Unfortunately, the weather did not permit such an attack until August, and by the time the assault finally took place, Tripoli had a navy of its own, including a brig, two schooners, two large galleys, and nineteen gunboats, the crews of which amounted to more than all those under Preble's command. The fight continued with all the ferocity of its beginning, and the enemy vessels, because of superior number of crew, chose to fight at close quarters, using pistols, sabers, pikes, and battle axes on both sides. Although it was a bloody battle, in the end, only one American officer was killed—the younger brother of Stephen Decatur, James, shot by a Tripolitan captain who had surrendered. While the enemy suffered heavy casualties both afloat and ashore, they withdrew indecisively. Four days later Preble and his squadron bombarded again and led an onshore attack on Tripoli. On this occasion none of the enemy's vessels advanced and there were no hand-to-hand encounters. Meanwhile, Preble continued the rigorous blockading under the uncounted difficulties of lack of adequate crews, lack of water, diminishing and insufficient stores, and scurvy. Three times he bombarded the Tripolitan enemy with all his guns. Preble's strict blockade policy and determination had their effect on the Bey of Tripoli, who began modifying his terms of ransom and for peace. Even so, Preble was disheartened, perhaps because he had news during these weeks of attacks on Tripoli that the Secretary of the Navy had ordered Captain Samuel Barron in the U.S. frigate *President* (Figure 2-15) to take command of his squadron.

In the late afternoon on September 9, 1804, *Constitution* was joined by the frigates *Constellation* and *President* with the new Commodore of the squadron, and Preble lowered his broad pennant on *Constitution*.

It was but three days later that this relieved flagship, at sometime after 4 a.m. on September 12, suffered humiliating damage. Amid light and

Figure 2-15. The U.S. frigate *President* was, until taken by the British, as valued by the Navy and the citizenry as *Constitution*. The ship's image in this painting, one of relatively few contemporary with the War of 1812, is convenient for comparing the two sisterships. This view shows *President* standing into the French naval base at Toulon in 1801. She is flying the broad pennant of the flagship of the Mediterranean squadron. Her deck and head arrangement are comparable to *Constitution*'s at this time.

baffling winds, *Constitution*, lying temporarily aback by veering winds and heading north-northeast, was struck by *President* standing to westward, *President*'s port bow striking *Constitution*'s bowsprit rigging and bow head. The two sister frigates lay afoul of each other, with *Constitution* swinging alongside as *President* continued under her own momentum with her sails still full and *Constitution*'s aback. They carried along, hung together by their two fouled anchors.

In this physical exchange, perhaps the only such between two American frigates, *Constitution* came off the worse, losing her head rigging, flying jibboom, jibboom, and part of her bowsprit, the original figurehead, and a critical part of her bow head, cutwater, and bow rails. Never again would her handsome forward profile be the same.

Captain Preble took *Constitution* to Syracuse, where he turned the ship over to young Captain Stephen Decatur, whose promotion had come through with the arrival of the new squadron command. Preble, in the meantime, arranged for his transportation to Naples and finally home in the small frigate *John Adams*. He had set a standard for the Tripolitan war that culminated in an acceptable peace with the release of hostages.

Captain Decatur was not long in command. Having just made the Captain rank, he was considered too "junior" to command such a large and prestigious ship, and was ordered on to other duties befitting an upwardly mobile young officer. In the meantime, the repair work on *Constitution* first took place at Malta, under the direction of Lieutenant Charles Gordon. Lasting from September 17, 1804, until November, these were major repairs—rebuilding the bow head and trailboards, re-rigging and partially restoring the bowsprit with a shorter spar assembly, replacing the destroyed figurehead with a carved billet or scroll head—carried out by Maltese workers who had neither the ship's original plans nor patterns for correct restoration.

Meanwhile, the squadron had been further reinforced with additional American warships. Captain John Rodgers was now in command, having taken over as the squadron's acting Commodore for sea operations at the request of the ailing Commodore Barron, who had taken up residence ashore in Syracuse. He had ordered *Constitution* to Lisbon, Portugal, for completion of the repairs and new anchors, and she left on November 14, once again the flagship as Rodgers hoisted his own broad pennant and returned in February to the Tripolitan shores. By May, the official negotiations for peace were underway.

Naval war with England: the outset

It may be arguable that the final peace treaty with Tripoli was a poor one. It could have resulted in total surrender if politics had not gotten in the way. Instead, the United States paid a $60,000 ransom for the captive crew of the USS *Philadelphia*. This treaty was signed on June 10, 1805, on board *Constitution*. The hostages all were returned immediately and taken on board the American squadron, and there would be no further tribute to the piratical Tripolitans.

Without Commodore Preble there would have been no treaty, but he was not there to see the fruits of his strategy. Had he been, doubtless he would have insisted on fewer conciliations. In one year his tight blockades, his persistent bombardments, and his rigid discipline on this station had engineered a reversal of Barbary attitudes. He had set the stage for all nations to enjoy legitimate seaborne trade in the Mediterranean without fear of attack by Barbary pirates. And all this had been orchestrated from the decks of USS *Constitution*.

The flagship, now under Commodore Rodgers, spent the winter of 1805–06 in Syracuse. Throughout the remainder of 1806 until June 1807, she cruised the Mediterranean under the command of Hugh Campbell, except for a three-month refit at a Lisbon shipyard, rated as being among the finest in Europe. Her hull and decks were completely recaulked, she received an entire new foremast as well as new standing rigging, and was fitted with new sails. Most probably, these repairs included some of the significant visual changes that she would carry into the coming conflict with the British Empire.

Before finally leaving the Mediterranean, *Constitution* had one more encounter with repairs. On her return to Syracuse, her rails and bow head, and the stern cabin windows, suffered heavy storm damage—enough to force her into Cagliari, the old port in Sardinia, for major repairs. She also stopped in Malta, and finally departed for Boston and home near the end of 1807, carrying a marble monument to Decatur, Somers, and the other heroes of Tripoli.

Meanwhile, on May 15, the Secretary of the Navy had ordered Captain James Barron, commanding USS *Chesapeake*, to depart Norfolk as soon as outfitted to relieve USS *Constitution* as flagship of the Mediterranean squadron. *Chesapeake* did not sail until June 22, when she was pressed to

Figure 2-16. The oldest and celebrated model of *Constitution*. Presented to Captain Isaac Hull by his crew after his successful cruises of 1812, the model was allegedly built by one of his crew, perhaps the ship's carpenter. Its value lies in its extensive detail, all of which is well worked out but not specifically well scaled. The story is told that, several years after presentation, it was used as a centerpiece for a banquet honoring Commodore John Rodgers, and the model's cannons were charged with powder and fuse. When they were fired in salute to Rodgers, they caused a small fire on the model that required repair. The model exists as shown, and the detail and proportions provide an authentic guide to her appearance in 1812. It was most useful in reconstructing the profile plan of Figure 2-22.

leave while still unready, her decks strewn with unstowed supplies, the new crew members unassigned to stations, and the ship altogether unprepared for sea.

Unfortunately, stationed near the mouth of Chesapeake Bay were two

Figure 2-17. A different view of the same model, showing deck arrangement. The craftsman-builder has concentrated heavily on the rigging and simplifies and omits much deck detail. For example, the guns are mounted on one-piece wooden blocks without trucks, trunions, or recoil gear. There seems to be no wheel, let alone double wheel helm, no mast boots or mast wedges, etc. Yet the rigging is replete with mousing on the stays, finely carved blocks, and deadeyes to the proper sizes. There are stun'sail booms, with their ring irons on yards as high as the topgallants. It is a most interesting and historic model.

British men-of-war. One of them, HMS *Leopard*, a 50-gun frigate, got underway and preceded the American frigate as she stood out to sea from Hampton Roads. As they fell into close company, the Britisher hailed Captain Barron and said that he had some dispatches for him. A boarding officer from *Leopard* produced a Royal Navy order to "stop and inspect" the American ship and to apprehend suspected deserters. This order having been rightly refused, the British lieutenant returned to his ship, which by then had been cleared for action. A few exchanged exhortations were lost in the wind—and then *Leopard* opened fire.

All was confusion on board *Chesapeake*, which was unready even for sea, let alone a broadside from a British frigate within sight of the Virginia capes. *Chesapeake*'s cluttered decks were now further littered with 23 casualties. Not only were the guns unloaded, but the gunners couldn't even find their firing matches. After firing one futile, protesting gun, Barron was forced to haul down his flag.

This, of course, became the celebrated *Chesapeake-Leopard* affair, which ultimately enraged the U.S. citizenry and astonished the President and Congress. There simply was no precedent for this near-piratical attack. No state of war existed between Britain and America. The British commander refused to acknowledge Captain Barron's surrender, but merely boarded his ship and took four men by force. *Chesapeake* struggled back to the Navy yard again for repair, and Captain Barron's career was placed at the mercy of a government investigation. And, as we shall see, this was not to be the last time that the U.S. frigate *Chesapeake* met defeat and dishonor before a British frigate—and for similar reasons.

The news of this international naval encounter reached *Constitution* in the small Spanish port of Malaga. Realizing that this affair could fan smoldering coals into fires of war, Captain Campbell took measures to strengthen his ship. As any good captain would, he put the ship on readiness alert—informing the crew, tightening the routine, and perhaps holding gun drills. At the time, she had been traveling with the brig-of-war *Hornet*, which was in his company. In August, in Gibraltar, Campbell received orders from the Secretary of Navy to close all naval activity in the Mediterranean and return to the United States. USS *Constitution* left in the company of USS *Wasp*, having dispatched *Hornet* to Malta and Syracuse to close all accounts still standing in those ports, which had been such loyal and reliable bases and supply yards.

The deplorable incident between *Chesapeake* and *Leopard* was in itself a microcosm of a problem existing throughout the maritime world. Since the close of the 18th century, the desperate struggle with the Napoleonic empire had become an extended war requiring nearly all of Britain's resources in men and war supplies. The Royal Navy, in particular, had become gigantic, and their burgeoning requirement for seamen fell heavily on the growing American merchant marine. A seaman's life in the British Navy was miserable. He was kept at sea for months and when in port kept on board without liberty, always with poor food and worse pay, and cruel floggings for even minor offenses. British seamen naturally found ways to desert. And this was not a desperate act of malcontents shirking their duty to King and Country; it was a driving need to get off a British warship at any costs, just to survive. And no other ships looked as inviting as American ships, where the pay was better and life was not threatening.

Admittedly, American merchant ships did carry in their crews some Royal Navy deserters. But these "deserters," many of whom became naturalized U.S. citizens, needed little encouragement to declare loyalty to the United States—a land newly independent from Great Britain, where all men were created equal. This made no difference to Royal Navy officers looking for crew; an American ship sailing in any ocean was a most attractive prey. British warships stopped any American merchant ship on the high seas and boarded them in foreign ports, taking off what crew they needed by calling them all deserters. So in 1807, when the British went so far as to stop and fire into an American warship at sea for *four* "deserters," two of whom proved to be native-born U.S. citizens, it became an international incident—an act of war. The British Navy later returned the two Americans seized from *Chesapeake*, and eventually apologized; as for the two Englishmen, they hanged one and allowed the other to die of his injuries. The American public mind long remembered this occasion.

Between 1807 and 1812 there was much agitated political maneuvering in the United States as well as between the warring nations France and England. In the U.S., increased westward expansion brought in new states with Congressional representatives who did not want to get entangled in international disputes. In short, there was much sharp contention toward mention of war. Congress and even the new President, James Madison, were still dominated by the Jeffersonian anti-Navy philosophy. Meanwhile, the British continued to impress American seamen into their warships, and passed "Orders in Council," a resolution that stalled all merchant trade by supporting British naval practices including impressment. Napoleon, for his part, countered with defiance of these British naval practices. None of these events encouraged a third country's participation in peaceful commerce.

At this time, American attitudes tended to favor France. There was continued trade with France; the captains of the smaller, faster American sailing vessels ignored the restrictive trade laws and ran British blockades of French ports.

There were further belligerent encounters between British and American warships. Near Cape Henry, about 45 miles off the entrance of the Chesapeake Bay, the U.S. frigate *President* encountered a strange ship in the night; requests for identification were answered with a cannonball that struck the American ship's mainmast. Captain Rodgers opened fire and after 15 minutes had rendered the defiant opponent unable to continue the exchange. The ship, which turned out to be the British sloop-of-war *Little Belt*, refused *President*'s offer of assistance and went off as best as her damaged rig and cut-up crew were able. This interchange did nothing to further British-American relations.

In late fall of 1811, President Madison called Congress into session. Angered by recent events, the President and Congress voted to increase the regular Army to 35,000 and suggested the Navy build 12 ships-of-the-line and 20 frigates to protect our coast. It was an enthusiastic, though unrealistic response to an emergency situation, given that one ship-of-the-line would take three to four years to build. At the very root of such preparedness fantasies on the part of Congress and the Madison administration was a complete ignorance of the global situation and naval affairs. Even the most cursory investigation would have shown them that the British Navy at this time consisted of 219 ships-of-the-line and 296 frigates. The United States Navy had but 16 serviceable warships, including the three heavy frigates, and not a single ship-of-the-line.

Nonetheless, on June 19, 1812, at the reluctant urging of President Madison, Congress declared war against Great Britain.

A question of performance

Constitution had not been idle in the time between returning from her four years in the Mediterranean until the declaration of war. She was involved in Navy peacetime duties, the more significant of which required carrying out diplomatic errands in Northern Europe, where she rubbed closely with the tempers and temperaments of the British and the French. Encounters over "deserters" and strained formal meetings with lofty and contemptuous British admirals provided her captain, Isaac Hull, and her crew the opportunity to experience the Royal Navy's overbearing attitude toward Americans. In late 1811, *Constitution* returned to the U.S. capital, proceeding to the Washington Navy Yard for a badly needed overhaul.

As the flagship of the Mediterranean fleet, *Constitution* was frequently loaded to her limits, carrying stores for other ships and for extended sea-keeping or blockade duty. She also suffered damage to her head rig, and evidence shows that her large foretriangle of staysails and jibs had been reduced, and probably not restored until she was at the end of her tour of duty in the Mediterranean. Also, the combination of the water's high salinity and the warm climate resulted in severe and rapid bottom fouling. In the Mediterranean, where only the larger shipyards could handle ships with *Constitution*'s deep draft (some 21 feet), there was little opportunity to careen such a large vessel for bottom cleaning. These factors all contributed to slow sailing and less-than-smart performance under sail.

So, when Captain Hull saw the opportunity in Washington Navy Yard, he looked at once toward a complete bottom cleaning. Unhappily, there was not enough copper sheathing available for a complete coppering job, but the ship was hove down and her bottom thoroughly cleaned and patched.

On June 18, 1812, the Secretary of Navy wrote to Captain Isaac Hull notifying him of the country's imminent state of war with Great Britain—and giving him instructions to join Commodore Rodgers's squadron in the Atlantic. At the time, *Constitution* was fresh out of the Washington Navy Yard, and Hull was still taking on stores, lying off Alexandria in the Potomac. But he sailed to Annapolis according to the Secretary's instructions to complete preparations for war and a long sea cruise. He also recruited seamen, carefully assessing each man's experience as he made assignments.

On July 4, Captain Hull was ready to sail, but being in no great rush, he joined in the nation's birthday celebrations, his national gun salute reverberating across the fields of Fort Severn and up the hill to the State House and back. The next morning, he ordered *Constitution* to weigh anchor, and, with the gun crews exercising, she sailed slowly down the bay.

Two days after *Constitution* sailed from her Annapolis anchorage, HMS *Bloodhound*, 10 guns, innocently sailed in and anchored—and was quickly boarded by Captain Gold, of a letter-of-marque schooner from Baltimore. *Bloodhound* was then taken over on Horn Point by a U.S. Army contingent from Fort Madison, much to the astonishment of her commander, Captain Rubridge, who had not heard of the declaration of war. *Bloodhound* had been carrying official dispatches, and was soon set free and allowed to sail, but not before 31 of her crew deserted, including an American seaman, young Robert Hyde, who had been impressed. Hyde's sad story of his cruel treatment appeared in the local newspaper and can be read today.[1]

It was a week before Captain Hull sailed out from the Virginia Capes. He realized it would be futile to try to catch up with the ships of Commodore Rodgers's squadron, which had sailed on June 22. Another reason to lag behind was that the Secretary of the Navy had mentioned that HMS *Belvidera* was in the Atlantic somewhere off the coast between New York and Virginia; *Constitution* cruised to the northeast in hopes of finding her. Unknown to Captain Hull, the British ship had barely escaped Commodore Rodgers's squadron a day out of New York, slipping away during the confusion after one of *President*'s main deck guns exploded. The Britisher sailed posthaste for Halifax, Nova Scotia, which was the principal Royal naval base in North America. There the ship notified Commodore Philip Broke in HMS *Shannon* that the United States was apparently at war with Britain. Broke, with his squadron of five ships, got underway at once and sailed for U.S. waters. It was, coincidentally, July 5, the same day that *Constitution* sailed from Annapolis.

On July 16, with Hull sailing a northerly course well offshore, beyond the latitude of Delaware Bay, *Constitution*'s first lieutenant noted in his journal,

. . . we discovered four vessels at great distance to the northwest and a single ship to the northeast, from which direction a light wind was blowing. The wind changed to the southward about sunset which brought us to windward, and we stood for the ship, the wind being very light. The [ship] was evidently a frigate and the first impression was that she might be a part of Commodore Rodgers's squadron.

The other ship was within hailing distance at about 11:00 p.m., and it was apparent she was not an American man-of-war. Both ships brought their heads to the wind and stood by until daylight.

The first light of day revealed to *Constitution*'s officers a large frigate within gunshot, and, within a mile or two on the lee quarter, a ship-of-the-line, three more frigates, and a brig, with a schooner astern of them. It was Broke's squadron, fresh from their Halifax base, now standing toward them with all sail set and flying English colors. This first real encounter with the enemy could well have been the end of our story. Captain Broke's flagship was HMS *Shannon*, a powerful frigate that, under his command, was within the year to meet and decimate the U.S. frigate *Chesapeake* in a humiliating 15-minute encounter off Boston.

In the confrontation of July 17, Captain Isaac Hull quickly assessed his situation, and while the nearest British frigate wasted 10 to 15 minutes wearing and tacking, he headed south and gained a little distance. By sunrise they found themselves becalmed, while the ships astern of them, still with a light breeze, were closing and near gunshot range. Hull hoisted out his longboats and rigged towlines, and by strenuous oar work began to keep their distance, as well as their sterns, from the enemy.

Soon the wind failed the British, and the pursuit became a great towing match. Hull took every reasonable action to maintain his lead—dumping several thousand gallons of fresh water to lighten ship, and sending the crew into the rigging with buckets to wet down the sails so that they would hold whatever breeze might blow—but the gap between *Constitution* and the British failed to widen; obviously Broke was determined to make a catch. Finally, Lieutenant Morris in *Constitution* suggested that in the past he had used anchors to kedge his way out of windless harbors. Captain Hull at once sounded the water and, finding over 20 fathoms, decided to try kedging. Although he lost a bit of distance in getting two anchors out and enough light hawsers rigged, their lead soon began to increase.

This contest lasted well into the next day, with occasional bits of breeze. The British ships experimented; the leading frigates furled their sails to reduce windage under their cumulative tows. Yet this seemed no great help. They could make three knots at times, but still not overtake *Constitution*. *Constitution* kept her sails rigged to take advantage of any moving air. At daylight on the second day, one enemy frigate was off *Constitution*'s port bow, but just out of gunshot range. The contest continued all that day and into the night. Ultimately, the wind steadied, and Captain Hull's ship pulled clear ahead and safely beyond his pursuers. This hair's-breadth chase lasted more than 60 hours, and in the end the American frigate demonstrated that under sail she could move faster than *any* of these five ships of the British Navy, four of them frigates and one a 74-gun ship-of-the-line. Doubtless Captain Hull was congratulating himself for having insisted on the recent thorough bottom cleaning.

Regardless, *Constitution*'s escape had humiliated a first-class British squadron and its commodore—from the vaunted Royal Navy. As Captain Hull said in self-deprecation, ". . . had they taken advantage of their early proximity and crippled me when in gunshot range, the outcome may have been different."

Frigate to frigate: *Constitution* and *Guerrière*

Constitution sailed on to Boston to check for any communication from Commodore Rodgers. Then, mindful that Broke's squadron was still at large (and fearing the remote possibility that a communication from the Navy Department might force him to relinquish his cherished command to a more senior captain), Captain Hull departed Boston on August 2.

Hull cruised briefly in the waters off Halifax and then turned southward toward the Bermudas. On August 18 he intercepted an American privateer, which reported seeing a British man-of-war standing southward the previous day. Hull sailed on without hesitation. On the afternoon of the next day, August 19, *Constitution*'s masthead lookout announced a sail on the horizon, bearing a little east of south. Two hours later the sail was identified as a large frigate sailing hard on the starboard tack on a south-westerly course. The wind was then in the northwest, and blowing a good 18 knots. As the ships closed, the stranger backed her mainsail and waited for *Constitution* to close. It proved to be a frigate from Broke's squadron, HMS *Guerrière*, under Captain Dacres, and he was anxious to fight.

The ships were well matched. *Constitution* carried a full crew and more than 50 guns; *Guerrière* had a smaller, but battle-experienced crew and 49 guns. Earlier, Captain Dacres had derisively challenged Captain Rodgers in *President* "or any other American frigate" to meet in a duel off Sandy Hook. He now had his chance.

The two ships maneuvered carefully for some 45 minutes, testing their guns' ranges and jockeying for position. Dacres then shortened sail, bearing up under topsails and jib alone, indicating a desire for close action. Hull, recognizing this challenge, steered directly for the British ship, at the same time ordering his gun crews to silence their batteries. As *Guerrière* opened vigorously with her long stern-chasers, Hull deliberately held his course, offering only a narrow target and enduring heavy fire, but loading his guns with double-shot and grape. As he finally veered into position about pistol range abreast of *Guerrière*, he ordered his gunners to open

Figure 2-18. A hand-colored lithograph, drawn by Baugean. It is a beautiful and accurately detailed work of art, depicting the famous contest of *Constitution* against *Guerrière*. The scene is depicted at the end, with *Constitution* backing off from the fatally crippled British "warrior" whose mainmast is about to go over. Note the several American sailors on the fore topgallant yard, apparently cheering.

fire. It was a full broadside—a direct blow from *Constitution* that fairly staggered her opponent. There was a hesitant recovery, but the well-drilled and eager American crews coolly reloaded and began a continuous and accurate fire. *Guerrière* responded—but the British crew never recovered their original aplomb and spirit. In half an hour, the British frigate lay helpless in the water (Figures 2-18 and 2-19), having abandoned the thought of saving the day with a boarding party in a heavy sea—and in the face of a determined company of American sailors and Marines.

Guerrière lay derelict and dismasted, while *Constitution* hauled into the wind ahead of her and took up position to rake—to send her full broadside

Figure 2-19. The defeat of *Guerrière* from another angle, showing *Constitution*'s engaged side. She is pouring her final broadside into the doomed enemy frigate. This lithograph is also engraved by Baugean.

crashing the length of the disabled British frigate. Captain Dacres wisely ordered a gun fired to leeward as a signal of surrender.

At this sign of capitulation, Captain Hull set fore and main sails on *Constitution* and sailed away to the east a few hundred yards to reorganize, repair damage, and, figuratively, brush herself off. Much of her running rigging was cut, some of the standing rig was shot up, and a few spars were splintered. After half an hour of hurried repairs, *Constitution* wore around and closed with *Guerrière*, now rolling helplessly in the trough with her gun deck awash. *Constitution*'s boat returned with Captain Dacres, who formally—with as much formality as his injured body and his more deeply injured pride would allow—surrendered.

The United States frigate *Constitution* had engaged a Royal Navy frigate in fair and direct ship-to-ship combat on the high seas and, in slightly more than an hour of actual maneuver and combat, had destroyed the enemy. It was the first major engagement of the naval war of 1812.

And it was during the most furious stage of this battle that a young American seaman standing near the ship's side was heard to say, as he watched a British cannonball bounce harmlessly off *Constitution*'s side, "Good God, her sides are made of iron!" Thus came her immortal name, "Old Ironsides."

Constitution returned to Boston with *Guerrière*'s prisoners. The news of the first real naval victory of this unpopular war was electrifying. Captain Isaac Hull and his ship and crew became immediate heroes, celebrated in the press not just locally but internationally. The *London Times* complained that this was the first time in history that an enemy frigate had defeated one of His Majesty's frigates in single combat. Captain Dacres' excuse—that Hull was lucky, and he would like a second chance at him—failed to impress the British Admiralty, and he was courtmartialed and found guilty of losing one of His Britanic Majesty's ships.

The greatest gain to the United States in this destruction of a significant British warship was the lift it gave the country's morale—not only of the people, but of the government. Just before the war, Congress had favored retiring the Navy's ships. It's doubtful that this sentiment would have prevailed; nevertheless, it indicates that there were many who felt the country was wrong in even having a navy, not to mention becoming involved at sea with an empire that ruled the seas. *Constitution*'s victory put to rest this sort of thinking, at least for a time. On the other hand, it might be said that *Constitution*'s victory obligated Americans to express their attitudes and position in world affairs—and that now they could enforce them.

Expressing the incident more simply, *Constitution* was victorious because a stronger ship with a skillfully trained crew met and defeated one less strong with a lesser crew. Perhaps this simple analytic truth was lost in the furor, but before war's end the British Admiralty issued instructions for

Royal Navy ships armed with 18-pounders to refuse or avoid battle when opposed by American 24-pounders.

Constitution and *Java*

Shortly after *Constitution*'s first victory, the U.S. Navy Department established a third squadron to cruise against British commerce. This was a small "tail-end" squadron, consisting of *Constitution*, 44; *Essex*, 36; and the sloop-of-war *Hornet*. *Constitution* served as flagship under the command of Captain William Bainbridge.

Constitution and *Hornet* left Boston on October 26, 1812, ordering *Essex*, then still fitting out in Philadelphia, to meet them in the Cape Verde Islands. *Essex* failed to arrive by the agreed-upon date, so *Constitution* and *Hornet* cruised together in the South Atlantic to coastal South America. Bainbridge left *Hornet* in Bahia, Brazil, to blockade a British merchant ship there. Three days after leaving Bahia, *Constitution* raised two sails on the horizon, a British frigate with an American prize. The prize was dispatched toward the nearest port, Bahia, and the two frigates squared away for battle. HMS *Java* was identified as the enemy and she held to her windward position.

Java was a new French frigate, captured by the British only a year before, and a fast sailer—an ability she used to advantage in the battle for best position. About an hour into this sailing match, a round shot smashed *Constitution*'s steering gear on deck; Bainbridge, who had been wounded in the hip by a musket ball as well as by a piece of flying metal debris from the steering wheel, was forced to rig jury steering two decks below. At about the same time, *Java* was hit in the head rig, bowsprit, and jibboom, losing her headsails and therefore any control in turning.

While *Java* luffed up into the wind, Bainbridge took the opportunity to close. *Constitution* wore around and passed under her stern, raking the helpless British frigate with a withering cannonade (Figure 2-21). Bainbridge wore ship again for a second raking broadside, but by now *Java*

Figure 2-20. HMS *Java* is ready to surrender as *Constitution* moves up to a threatening raking position astern. The American commander is hailing through a speaking trumpet on the forecastle, as is his British counterpart on the port side of his quarter deck. This excellent, detailed lithograph is drawn by an artist signing only "W.G.," noting that the scene is drawn "under the direction of a witness to the action."

had lost her foremast and was unable to maneuver into any position. Bainbridge sailed around her in a commanding position. *Java* put up a valiant defense, but could not withstand the heavy broadsides at such close range, and was soon completely dismasted. Captain Lambert had been mortally wounded by a musket ball from *Constitution*'s Marine sharpshooters in the maintop. Bainbridge withdrew to repair damaged rigging, assuming that *Java* had surrendered—her flag was in the water with the fallen masts and rigging debris—but Lambert's first lieutenant attempted

Figure 2-21. Another aspect of the final stroke against HMS *Java*, as her mainmast falls; this was after Figure 2-20's scene in which *Constitution* returned after lying off, assuming *Java* had surrendered. The engraving is by Baugean.

to continue the already lost battle. When Bainbridge returned to accept surrender, he discovered his opponent's colors had been recovered and were flying on a rigged-up pole, but when *Constitution* took up a raking position ahead of *Java*, she struck her flag at once. The contest ended less than four hours after it began.

The British frigate was so riddled with gunfire that she was beyond saving; Bainbridge ordered her fired, and her powder room blew up; the only thing salvaged was her wheel, which Bainbridge took to replace *Constitution*'s, smashed early in the contest. For many years this wheel served *Constitution* as a useful replacement and a badge of victory.

Bainbridge rendezvoused with *Hornet*, and ordered her to remain behind to continue the blockade of the rich British merchant ship in Bahia. Feeling his own wounds and the wounds of his ship, he decided to return home, rejoicing in the thought of the report he'd make: another victory for *Constitution*—and a relatively new ship, equal in armament and size to *Guerrière*. Recalling that celebration, he envisioned something similar in his honor. Congress had struck special medals and appropriated $50,000 as prize money; they might do as much again. After all, his victory was only the second such frigate-to-frigate victory.

Bainbridge would soon learn from an American brig during his return trip, however, that his conquest was the third and not the second victory for the American frigates. At about the same time as Bainbridge's cruise began, Captain Stephen Decatur, in the sister frigate *United States*, had met with HMS *Macedonian*—a formidable 38-gun frigate, considered one of the finest in her class, fresh out of drydock, and only two years old—near the Canary Islands. After three hours of a massive exchange of gunfire, Decatur had rendered this powerful ship a helpless, mastless wreck; nonetheless, he was determined to return with his prize, and spent two weeks returning *Macedonian* to sailing condition. At risk of being recaptured by the various Royal Navy squadrons cruising about the North Atlantic, Decatur sailed nearly 4,000 miles and brought his prize unharmed into New York.

Although Decatur's triumph somewhat dampened the victorious return of Bainbridge in *Constitution*, the fact remained that in this first year of war, American frigates had met on three occasions and had unquestionably vanquished three British frigates. This sent a troubling message to Great Britain, and swung American public opinion enthusiastically behind the war. It was not in any way a serious challenge to the unquestioned British naval superiority, however. The British Empire was embroiled in a destructive war with Napoleon and his expansive threat to the European continent, and although the British were prevailing, that war would not be finally settled for three more years. This naval contest with the upstart former colony was simply a frustration—the loss of three frigates among their several hundred was no blow to their naval power.

The British Admiralty—in a tactical retreat—ordered its command at sea to direct all frigates to cease engaging superior American frigates in single combat. They then reinforced their blockading squadrons in American waters, isolating the movement of these "superior" frigates. Up to the end of 1812, only two of the heavy *Constitution*-class frigates had been able to engage in ship-to-ship duels, but this was enough to astonish the British and to justify the wisdom of the design choices made by their creator, Joshua Humphreys.

The final blockade: *Cyane* and *Levant*

After the *Java* victory and celebration, *Constitution* returned to Boston for a complete yard overhaul, reconstruction of battle damage, and the replacement of deteriorating wood. Near the end of this overhaul, Captain Bainbridge was relieved by Captain Charles Stewart. Stewart had seen service in the Mediterranean as a senior officer in the squadron with Commodore Preble, had served on the sister frigate *United States*, and had commanded several smaller ships. He was a seasoned and competent officer. This was his first command of a larger frigate, although he had been ordered to *Constellation* but never got her to sea because of the intensive British blockade around Norfolk. He was understandably pleased to move aboard *Constitution*, just finishing her overhaul in Boston, where the blockade was easier to deal with.

It was the end of December when Stewart cleared for sea on *Constitution*'s next war cruise—bound for the Caribbean where British merchantmen were known to be trading. But the British merchant trade—knowing they were at risk of being taken by one of the abundant American privateers or a United States naval vessel—were traveling in escorted convoys. Seeking better hunting, Stewart headed south to the South American coast but again did not engage in battle. One possible encounter with a British 36-gun frigate ended with the escape of the frigate in light, variable winds. Now, because of a crack developing in the ship's mainmast, Stewart decided to return to Boston for repair, near which he had the ill-timed luck of encountering two British 38s in company and appearing ready for action. Stewart thought the safest and wisest choice would be a run into Marblehead Harbor, where he anchored. A few days later *Constitution* was underway again and, in the temporary absence of blockading ships, made Boston Harbor.

The subsequent blockade of Boston Harbor soon after *Constitution*'s arrival made it apparent that British frigates were now traveling in company, and the extent and strength of the blockade was spreading. *Constitution* had returned in early April, and by May 7 the blockade extended to Portsmouth, New Hampshire, where lay another U.S. frigate, *Congress*. By the end of May, the three English frigates covering the area between Cape Cod and Cape Ann were joined by the impressive ship-of-the-line HMS *Ramillies*, flying the flag of Rear Admiral Thomas M. Hardy, Lord Nelson's former captain at Trafalgar. The frustrated Captain Stewart found himself trapped again.

Stewart was perhaps the most aggressive of all the War of 1812 captains, and he was impatient to get to sea. At the first sign of relaxation in the blockade, he was off. It so happened that the British *had* temporarily "looked the other way"—three of the blockading ships were off to Halifax for stores and renewal, and a fourth one was trying to cover too much coastline. When the British became aware that their prize quarry was missing from Boston, *Constitution* was on her way well to the south.

Stewart fruitlessly cruised the seas from Bermuda to Tobago, taking an English merchant prize bound for Liverpool and checking other merchant vessels for information. One prize taken off the Portuguese coast rewarded *Constitution* with what historical sources only refer to as unspecified "valuable cargo." A short time after this, Stewart expected there would be a reaction from the Royal Navy base in Gibraltar. Several days later he raised two sails on the horizon. The weather was light and the sea state good as the two British men-of-war—a light frigate, 34 guns, and a corvette, armed with 22 guns, mostly 32-pound carronades—closed with

Constitution. The two lighter vessels against the heavy American frigate made for an interesting match.

It was February 20, 1815. The British opened fire first, at about sunset. The first shot smashed one of *Constitution*'s boats; there would be little further damage. Stewart's tactical maneuvering of *Constitution* in this engagement was remarkable: he kept the two enemy ships separated and unable to combine their strength, while at the same time continually bringing *Constitution* in range and in the most threatening position—on one occasion even backing his ship for tactical advantage. Several times, Stewart successfully brought the two British ships separately under his heavy raking fire. Finally, within an hour, he accepted the surrender of the frigate, HMS *Cyane*. After exchanging broadsides in passing, the new corvette HMS *Levant* had to be chased for nearly two hours of hot pursuit before *Constitution* was close enough to disable her and bring her to surrender.

Unknown to the combatants, representatives of the United States and Great Britain had met in Ghent, Belgium, to discuss terms of peace; a treaty was signed on Christmas Eve, 1814, and ratified February 18, 1815. President Madison proclaimed the war with Britain at an end. But news traveled slowly at this time in history. Prizes would still be taken by privateers and guns would still be fired in anger for weeks to come—including the American victory at New Orleans. But for "Old Ironsides," this was her last great battle during the War of 1812. She set sail for home, stopping in Brazil to put her prisoners ashore, then sailed on to the Caribbean where, in Puerto Rico, the crew learned of the peace treaty's ratification. Because of the difficulties of communication, the treaty granted a 30-day grace period; consequently, *Constitution*'s conquest of *Cyane* and *Levant* had been valid according to international agreement.

Captain Stewart set course for New York, where he arrived on May 15 to a reception the equal of those accorded Hull and Bainbridge. *Constitution* was renowned as a superior warship with three substantial victories and no defeats. Her tough sides and heavy guns that shattered enemy frigates;

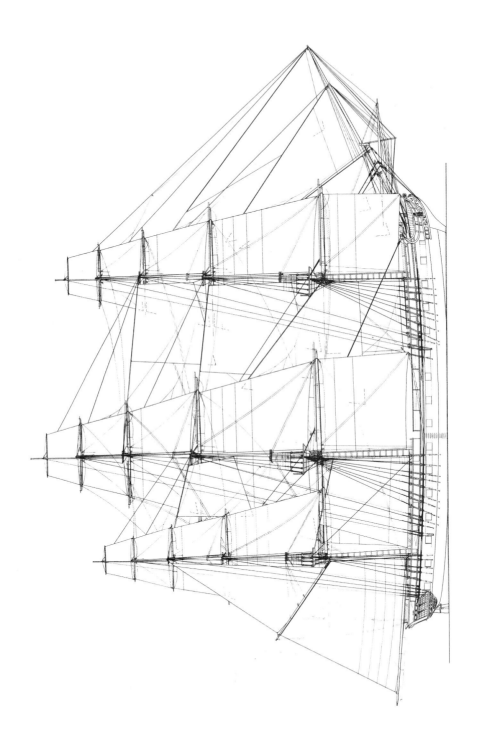

her veteran crew, nearly all hand picked; and her commanders—Hull, Bainbridge, and Stewart—had made *Constitution* famous, and earned her a brilliant place of national honor.

The battle score for the U.S. Navy's frigates, the hardest-hitting of the Navy's ships, stood at four victories to one loss. In three major engagements, *Constitution* had taken four ships and *United States* one. And although the luckless *Chesapeake* had been shamefully defeated in 15 minutes by the veteran Captain Broke in HMS *Shannon*, the American frigates' celebrated battle records had more bearing on national morale than any other victory in the War of 1812.

Strategically, however, Oliver Hazard Perry's victories in 1813 on Lake Erie and Lake Champlain were much more significant. The loss of five of His Majesty's warships was, in fact, almost nothing to the British Navy, except as a blow to the pride of the several captains and crews. The strength of British seapower remained intact, and Britain's vast fleets continued the blockade of all of Europe and the patrol of the world's sea lanes. But for those American citizens who were aware—and who among them could not be?—the United States of America had now proved they were no longer subservient to the British Empire. They were now a nation among nations whose ships could stand against an equal enemy with a better than equal chance of winning. The U.S. Navy had justified itself within the halls of government and for the President's concerns. The Navy now had a permanent place in the armed forces.

Figure 2-22. The U.S. frigate *Constitution* as she most likely appeared at the apogee of her career. By this date, 1812–15, she carried the maximum sail. Her topgallant masts carried sky-poles, and while this plan does not show her lighter sails such as stun'sails, ring tail, water sails, and the rest, her stun'sail booms are apparent at the ends of her yards.

LIST OF AMERICAN NAVY SHIPS—JUNE 27, 1812

Name	Rated	Guns Mounted	Command
FRIGATES			
Constitution	44	55	Capt. Isaac Hull
United States	44	55	Capt. Stephen Decatur
President	44	55	Commodore John Rodgers
Chesapeake	36	44	(not in commission)
New York	36	44	(not in commission)
Constellation	36	44	Captain William Bainbridge (outfitting)
Congress	36	44	Capt. Moses Smith
Boston	32	—	(not in commission)
Essex	32	—	Capt. David Porter
Adams	32	—	(not in commission)
CORVETTE			
John Adams	26	—	Capt. Augustus Ludlow

Name	Rated	Guns Mounted	Command
SLOOPS-OF-WAR			
Wasp	16	18	Capt. Jones
Hornet	16	18	Capt. James Lawrence
BRIGS			
Siren	16	—	Lt. Carroll
Argus	16	—	Lt. Crane
Oneida	16	—	Lt. Woolsey
SCHOONERS			
Vixen	12	—	Lt. Gadsen
Nautilus	12	—	Lt. Sinclair
Enterprise	12	—	Lt. Blakely
Viper	12	—	Lt. J. Bainbridge
170 Gunboats		20	at New Orleans

3

Peace, Cruises, Idleness, and Neglect

Upon returning in 1815 to her home port in Boston, *Constitution* was received by an old friend and former Commander—Captain Isaac Hull, now the Commandant of the Charlestown Navy Yard, where she was to be overhauled to prepare for another Mediterranean cruise. While American warships were occupied by the war with Britain, the Bey of Algiers had returned to piracy, seizing American merchant ships and crews. A squadron of ships under Captain Stephen Decatur, commanding a new frigate named *Guerrière*, was sent to force an end to this state-sponsored piracy. After Decatur sank the Algerian flagship *Mashuda*, he sailed into Algiers and forced terms "at the mouth of our cannon." Faced with a superior American force, the Bey had no choice but capitulation. When word came back of Decatur's success, *Constitution*'s Mediterranean cruise was canceled. In 1815, with the expectation of peace and prosperity, *Constitution* was laid up—sadly and to no advantage to her structural health—for nearly five years.

Peacetime layup—and buildup

For some perspective on these years of "peace and prosperity" that led to *Constitution*'s five-year layup, let us again take a broader view of the Western world of the day. The "American" War of 1812, which we have followed through the career of only one warship, was an isolated conflict having little connection with European activity—and little significance. The all-consuming conflict involved Napoleon's continued domination of most of the European continent.

By 1812, Napoleon or his family and allies ruled almost all of Europe. He had defeated Prussian armies, Russian armies, and squelched resistance in Austria and Spain in 1805–09; Italy was his in 1800. And although Admiral Nelson had destroyed Napoleon's sea power at Trafalgar in 1805, this little man, now a self-proclaimed emperor, had under his command the greatest military machine ever assembled, perhaps since Genghis Khan. In June 1812, he set out with some 600,000 troops on a magnificently ill-prepared conquest of all the Russias, beginning with a march on Moscow. What he hoped would be his greatest quest, however, turned into ignominious defeat six months later. His retreat from an abandoned Moscow in that terrible winter of 1813 led to the subsequent defeat of his decimated armies—by then reduced to only 10,000 men—by the Prussians at the Battle of Leipzig. Betrayed and deserted by his allies, Napoleon was forced to abdicate in April 1814.

It was a gentleman's abdication, however, and Napoleon was exiled to the Mediterranean island of Elba—still, in his own egocentric mind, the emperor; and still with many friends and enthusiastic followers in France.

The British and the Prussians, once allied against Napoleon, were now at odds, and the puppet government in Paris was in disarray. To the "emperor" on Elba, this was irresistible. His landing at Antibes on the provincial Mediterranean coast was followed quickly by a triumphant return to a jubilant Paris, but his reign lasted only 100 days before his defeat by Wellington at Waterloo. This time his exile was to be *truly* exile—on lonely, remote St. Helena, a volcanic island in the South Atlantic.

Throughout this first decade-and-a-half of the 19th century, continental Europe and the British Empire had known virtually nothing but non-stop war, and had paid little attention to the fledgling United States across the Western ocean.

The so-called "Pax Britannia" that followed Napoleon's defeat was an era that belonged to the British Empire and her naval might, although other nations basked in the partial sun provided by Britain's peace. For the United States, too, it was a time of peace, and peacetime is a hard time for laid-up warships. If the peace is long enough, they almost never survive. The United States saw three full decades without a shooting conflict.

The peacetime Navy and the government politicians were not long in preparing for the bureaucratic domination of their realm. Before 1815 was through, Congress established a Board of Navy Commissioners to serve under the Secretary of the Navy. In April 1816, Congress ordered a gradual "increase in the Navy." This was, in fact, a step to prevent selling off the ships and to prevent the naval establishment from withering away, as had happened after the revolution. *Constitution* and her successes had largely justified this new Congressional enthusiasm for the Navy.

The new ships authorized in 1816 were to be ships-of-the-line, battleships named after states—the beginning of a long tradition. Unfortunately, little consideration was given to their cost or intricate construction, their maintenance and manning, or their use.

Ships-of-the-line were a nation's heavyweight battleships. They were literally floating fortresses with an astonishing ability to propel barrages of heavy iron balls at objects of like kind—force against force. In the case of the British against America in the War of 1812, ships-of-the-line were also quite effective at blockading harbors.

When I was a midshipman studying naval tactics and strategy of battleships' formation, I often wondered what would happen if the enemy did not want to fight with battleships in formations or with battleships at all.

The answer came in the Second World War. After literally losing all our battle-line ships at Pearl Harbor, we were, in fact, forced to fight the great Pacific naval war against a Japanese Navy using a new strategy. This led to our reliance on aircraft carriers escorted by heavy cruisers and the new super *Iowa*-class battleships, which together formed the state-of-the-art tactical machine called a "Task Force." It marked the end of the centuries-old floating fortress mentality.

After the War of 1812, however, ships-of-the-line were still very much in vogue, and the U.S. Congress was all too eager to embrace them. The desire for these ships was based in part on past heroic victories—such as Nelson's at Trafalgar—which were very visible signatures of sea power.

You will recall from Chapter One that the term "ship-of-the-line" is part of the historic nomenclature for sailing ships. The term had its origins in the late 17th century, but by the end of the 18th century the categories of ships-of-the-line in Britain's Royal Navy included four different "rates" larger than frigates (see Figure 1-1). The most popular ship-of-the-line in 1800 was a third-rate ship of 74 guns, with two gun decks.

On paper, these third-rate ships seemed ideal for the U.S. Navy. They carried more hitting power than a frigate such as *Constitution*, and, while heavier, they were still shapely enough to be maneuverable, and could carry enough sail to be nearly as fast. Congress, no doubt, felt that such ships would be the backbone of the nation's sea power. Then it took this concept to its furthest degree and ordered some 100-gun first rates. But these were tremendously complex wooden structures with layered gun decks, built of the most durable and expensive timber. Building a ship-of-the-line in 1816 would require a serious outlay of resources. A first-rate ship alone would need about five times the material resources as a frigate like *Constitution*. Timber of adequate dimensions for the ship's backbone and frame would necessarily come from trees at least 100 years old—and a first rate would require some 1,000 of them. Years of ship construction—the arms race of the 18th and 19th centuries—meant that such trees were not readily available. At the end of the 18th century, the Royal Navy depended on oak from the Baltic countries. While English shipwrights were critical of using anything but native wood, they also learned to be partial to American oak from the forests of the Northeast. During the War for Independence, the British were temporarily shut off from Northeast timber. They returned again, however, after peace was restored. For years afterwards, their timber-carrying ships maintained a nearly continuous caravan of shipbuilding timber between New England and Great Britain. This lasted until the first decade of the 19th century when international relations once again deteriorated. In short, by 1816, American oak suitable for the proposed American ships-of-the-line was already becoming expensive.

Nevertheless, after 1815, the Navy proceeded to plan and build some ships-of-the-line called "liners." The first was USS *Delaware*, laid down in 1817 and launched in 1820 in Norfolk, Virginia. She was followed by *North Carolina*, launched in 1820 in Philadelphia.

The expanding naval armament began to cool a bit by 1818 when four more 74s were laid down; the earliest of these to be launched was *Vermont*, keel laid 1818, launched 1845. And, almost unbelievably, a 120-gun ship-of-the-line, USS *Pennsylvania*, was laid down in 1822. As if to prove the complexity and expense of such an undertaking, she was not completed until 1837.

One may question what type of military/political combo conceived and authorized such powerful ships in a time of peace. Indeed, it is difficult to resist comparing today's failed B-2 Bomber project with the Navy's ships-of-the-line in the period following the War of 1812. The Navy certainly did not need these large, unwieldy, Nelsonian turtles with which Congress had been so enamored. These floating fortresses were better suited for European nations where short coastlines reduced the need for mobility. America would have been better served by the mobility and effectiveness of frigates such as *Constitution*. In fact, the naval operational command did retain such ships. After all, they had proved their value.

The bottom line is that Congress liked these large symbols and hoped they'd be an effective response to the British blockade of the United States coastal ports in the War of 1812. These ships would not permit such an embarrassment to be repeated—or would they?

The story of the ships-of-the-line in the U.S. Navy is a sad but familiar tale of wasteful defense projects conceived by politicians. *Columbus*, *Franklin*, *Washington*, and *Independence* were authorized and laid down during the War of 1812, but none saw action. All fell short of expectations structurally—the naval constructors having had no experience with such monster floating fortresses. Of the three completed shortly after the war—*Ohio*, *Delaware*, and *North Carolina*—only *Ohio* was a successful ship. Others, such as *Vermont*, laid down in 1818 but not completed until 1845, were difficult to keep from decaying on the building stocks as they were nearly abandoned on the ways. The largest of all these great fortresses was the USS *Pennsylvania*, 120 guns, laid down in 1822. Larger than any European ship-of-the-line, she occupied the entire labor force in the Philadelphia Navy Yard. After an undistinguished life as a coastal defense ship (against no enemy), she was burned in Norfolk Navy Yard in 1861.

The Mediterranean revisited

In May 1821, the recommissioned *Constitution*, now under Captain Jacob Jones, sailed for Gibraltar, once again to become the flagship of the Mediterranean squadron. It was here that she also met with a new 74-gun ship-of-the-line, USS *Columbus*, under the command of Commodore Charles Stewart.[1]

Constitution arrived at her new base at Port Mahon in Minorca, the Balearic Islands, in June 1821—an ideal time to cruise the peaceful Mediterranean, with Europe recovering from the Napoleonic Wars. For *Constitution*, this tour in the Mediterranean—as flagship part of the time and subordinate part of the time—involved no action more dangerous than diplomatic support and showing the flag in ports from Tangier to the Dardanelles. She returned briefly to New York in the summer of 1824 for a turnover of officers and crew and a brief, minor overhaul—rigging renewal, replenishment, and some rig modifications on fore and main.[2] There were no structural changes.

Constitution returned to the Mediterranean under Captain Thomas Macdonough's command. Macdonough took his squadron to Sicily and Syracuse where he planned to await further orders from Commodore John Rodgers, who was to take command of the squadron from the decks of a new flagship—a 74-gun ship-of-the-line, USS *North Carolina*. Rodgers's command was largely for a diplomatic peace-keeping mission in Turkey, where he had been ordered to meet with the Turkish Minister of Marine to sign a treaty furthering better relations between their countries' maritime industries. They departed Gibraltar as a newly constituted squadron on July 9, 1825. *Constitution* continued this duty under an exchange of commanding officers and new captains until after the winter of 1827–28. Under the command of a new Commodore, Daniel Patterson, she was ordered home. *Constitution* arrived home in Boston on July 4, 1828.

Constitution's first major restoration, 1833–35

Back in Boston, *Constitution* was becoming a venerable old monument at the age of 31 years. Whether this is young or old for a wooden ship is arguable. Some vessels built hurriedly for war service in 1812, particularly privateers, were built, launched, and fitted out in a few months—obviously intended to be short-term investments in a relatively short war. Built of less durable woods and cheap fittings, they were serviceable for about two to three years. In contrast, the original six frigates authorized in 1794 were well designed and well built, as evidenced by the sobriquet "Old Ironsides." *Constitution* had "been through the wars," however, and seen the roughest of service; even so, she had been relatively well cared for, with four to five major and minor yard overhauls, not to mention the sundry repairs in foreign stations. For a well-built wooden ship, or a smaller wooden vessel such as a yacht, 31 years normally would be considered late middle age—not time to be summarily condemned, but time to have a thorough physical examination. Consequently, the Secretary of the Navy ordered a complete survey of *Constitution*, and the Navy Board of Commissioners also conducted its own survey.

These lengthy and exhaustive surveys were complete with cost figures for necessary repair and restorations. Somewhere along the line, these costs became publicly known, and an astonishing amount of concern was given to making comparisons to new-ship costs. Whether to replace *Constitution* with a new vessel or order the extensive reconstruction became a media topic. The Navy, however, had made no decision, despite rumors to the contrary that *Constitution* had been condemned.

The public concern at this time—a surprise to the Navy Commissioners and the Secretary—was further aroused by the publication of Oliver Wendell Holmes's now-famous poem, "Old Ironsides," which praised *Constitution*'s exploits and bemoaned her neglect, as if she had already been discarded.

This poem first appeared in the *Advertiser*, a Boston newspaper that had taken up the first media defense of *Constitution* and was sounding the alarm at the presumed threat of the famous ship's condemnation. The alarm spread through other cities' newspapers, and the poem was printed and reprinted until restoration of the ship became a national cause. The Navy Department was quick to react to the popular feeling, and the order was promptly dispatched to the Charlestown Navy Yard in Boston to proceed with the repair of "Old Ironsides."

OLD IRONSIDES

by Oliver Wendell Holmes

Ay, tear her tattered ensign down!
Long has it waved on high,
And many an eye has danced to see
That banner in the sky;
Beneath it rung the battle shout,
And burst the cannon's roar;—

The meteor of the ocean air
        Shall sweep the clouds no more.
Her deck, once red with heroes' blood,
        Where knelt the vanquished foe,
When winds were hurrying o'er the flood,
        And waves were white below,
No more shall feel the victor's tread,
        Or know the conquered knee;—
The harpies of the shore shall pluck,
        The eagle of the sea!
Oh, better that her shattered hulk
        Should sink beneath the wave;
Her thunders shook the mighty deep,
        And there should be her grave;
Nail to the mast her holy flag,
        Set every threadbare sail,
And give her to the god of storms,
        The lightning and the gale

The repairs, authorized in February 1831, were to be extensive. The Navy yard noted at this time that the ship showed considerable hogging and the hull was altered from "the original lines." Captain Morris, commandant of the Navy yard, argued rightfully that the structural repairs should be delayed until the new drydock, the Navy's first and currently under construction, was completed. He felt the ship was not strong enough to withstand the conventional "heaving down" for bottom repairs.

Unfortunately, from 1829 to 1833, amid endemic indecision and bureaucratic delays in the construction of the drydock, the idle frigate continued to deteriorate, for a ship laid up is far more vulnerable to deterioration than a ship in full commission, populated by a large lively crew working at sea. By April 1833 her fittings and interior gear were stripped off and she was under a protective roof, ready for drydock service.

The directives for repair called for new hull planking on both sides from below the wales to the main rail; new ceiling (the heavy interior planking inside the frames) in the hold; new deck beams under the orlop (a ship's lowest deck) and berth decks as well as new deck planking and new weather deck (spar deck) planking; new quarter galleries and channels; new knight-heads and repairs to stem and head; recaulking throughout; and recoppering of the bottom.

Nothing was said in the directives concerning the gun-deck beams—a ship's largest, heaviest, and most structurally significant deck timbers. The gun deck is essentially the main strength deck, serving much like the top of a long box girder; the beams and the decking are of individually greater size than their counterparts in the spar, berth, and orlop decks. Also, nothing was said in the directives about restoring or repairing the frames—the rib-like, heavy, curving timbers between the outer planking skin and the inner ceiling, the most important factor in her transverse strength. The survey report mentioned the frames as being sound—although it is difficult to imagine how they were *all* examined, particularly in the bottom, without removing ceiling, planking, or both. Further, nothing was said concerning the below-water fastenings, although we may well presume that they were sound, being of heavy copper.[3] All rigging, sails, as well as all three masts and spars, were to be replaced—and that is no small item.

The first cost estimate was increased two or three times and finally settled in at a projected $158,000. This 1830 figure seems relatively low next to today's Defense Department budget, where a new aircraft carrier might project into ten figures, not including the inevitable cost overruns. The inflated dollar is not the only bad basis for such comparison; there is also the complexity of today's state-of-the-art technology, and the far greater size of the modern warship. The simple base for estimating ship cost is on a weight basis. *Constitution*'s weight (load waterline) was 2,200 long tons. The old frigate's repair cost on this basis was estimated at less than $72 per ton, compared to her new-ship cost in 1797 of approximately $303,000 or $137 per ton. Apparently her restoration estimates were grossly under cost, or the claim by officials and others who said it would be cheaper to build a new ship was grossly exaggerated.

By June 1833, with all the public concern and debate, *Constitution* had become such a *cause célèbre* that distinguished citizens came from far and near to see the dedication of the new drydock in Boston's Navy Yard where the venerable "Old Ironsides" would be given a new life. President Andrew Jackson had begged off traveling to Boston because of poor health, but he was represented by Vice President Martin Van Buren together with the Secretary of the Navy, the Secretary of War, and the Governor of Massachusetts. The famous, though aging, Commodore Isaac Hull was given temporary command of the yard for the docking procedure, which went off most successfully.

Let me emphasize that *Constitution* had never before undergone such a thorough overhaul. As a matter of semantics we must refer to this occasion in 1833–35 as her first major restoration.

Up until this time *Constitution* had undergone ten significant maintenance overhauls:

1803	Boston*	New rigging and mainmast repaired
1804	Malta	Bowhead rebuilt, carronades added, ship repainted
1808–09	New York	Upper planking repaired
1812	Washington*	New mainmast, mainmast components, new bowsprit and stemhead
1813	Boston*	New ceiling planking above gundeck
1820–21	Boston*	New planking above wales, some beams and knees renewed
1822	Port Mahon (Mediterranean)	Mainmast repair
1823	Port Mahon	Main and mizzenmast repair
1824	New York	Rigging changes; no structural work; head and stem restored
1825	Port Mahon	Thorough caulking inside and out

* Hove down for bottom cleaning and restoring copper.

While *Constitution* spent considerable time in the shipyard at Port Mahon in Minorca from 1825 to 1828, this was not for heavy-overhaul work. Also, it is difficult to justify from the records any serious overhaul in 1824 in New York. So it should be better said that the ship, in her 31 years of active service, had been given only seven or fewer complete overhauls.

Of course, the frigate had been maintained, and after accidents and battle damages she had been repaired either at sea or in the most convenient port. The most extensive of these repairs were in Malta, Gibraltar, Lisbon, and Syracuse. As we have seen in Chapter Two, the most extensive repairs had been carried out at Malta in 1804 after her collision with *President*. The stemhead was rebuilt, but local carpenters had worked without plans or patterns, and the new trailboards and billethead reportedly lacked the expertise of a professional shipcarver or carpenters skilled in that sort of work; the bowsprit and jibboom were also replaced hurriedly and with some clumsiness. Four years later, after the headrails had washed away at sea, this new head configuration was refined in New York by a craftsman named Daniel Train. Train largely replaced the decorative details, including an artfully carved new billethead, quarter gallery, and renewed stem decorations. Between these two reconstructions, the bow area was considerably changed. And this would not be the last of it.

In the 1833 Boston docking and subsequent extensive overhaul, the primary concern was restoring the hull shape—namely, the hogging condition. "Hogging" describes the distortion of a hull when the ends of the ship have subsided below the middle. Inasmuch as the keel and backbone structure are centrally involved, the restoration work is concentrated there. According to the survey, *Constitution*'s hogging condition was evident in 1833. It is reported that after she was refloated, the hogging condition had been corrected. This may have been so; the records of the restoration are not particularly specific. There is no record of corrective rider frames being installed in the inner bottom area or below the orlop in the middle body, and we must assume that they were never there before or after. Although the hogging may have been temporarily removed or improved, it would soon return—as it would thereafter whenever *Constitution* approached another overhaul or restoration, even at this writing. I will discuss this in greater detail in the chapters to come.

Once the structural work was completed, "Old Ironsides" was redecorated with a new white gunstripe carried forward around the stemhead, and a new, controversial figurehead—a life-size statue of then-President Andrew Jackson. The entire redecoration project was undertaken by Captain Jesse D. Elliott, Commodore Bainbridge's replacement; in fact, it was Elliott who generated the changes to the forward end of the ship. Apparently there were no carved head rails or trailboards at this date.

The new figurehead, carved less than skillfully, caused quite a ruckus. President Jackson was a popular President, but he still had his detractors—on the left and right—who did not want to see his image on the nation's most popular warship. Protests ensued. Debate reverberated in the halls of Congress In the meantime, someone snuck onto *Constitution* after dark and beheaded the new figurehead. Absurdly, it was this headless figure, already installed, that *Constitution* would carry with her. In light of these events, we can briefly say that Captain Elliott was not a person of sensitive persuasion or an artistic eye. He presided over a ludicrous period in the otherwise dignified life of the country's favorite warship, as we will see in the following pages.

Constitution was ready for sea in the spring of 1835. She sailed for New York in March 1835, with Captain Elliott now as the ship's commander.

A flagship for diplomacy

For nearly the next ten years, *Constitution* served the Navy on diplomatic errands as flagship of various squadrons, encountering extremely heavy seas and weather, including an exceptionally rough handling by a hurricane. Under the command of Commodore Elliott until 1838, she continued to suffer the indignities of his fertile and arrogant mind. During his tour of duty, this self-serving man conducted the activities of the ship according to his own whims. He perceived the ship as his personal habitat, much as his private yacht or transport. While in the Mediterranean, he collected "artifacts," filling the hold with statuary, vases, stone columns, marble sarcophagi, even an Egyptian mummy, among other antiquities. Before setting sail to return to the United States from Mediterranean duty, he embarked enough farm animals to stock a medium-sized farm, converting the gun deck into an extensive stable. The ship was called "Elliott's Ark" by her crew. There were six mules, nine Arabian horses plus one Spanish horse, three Spanish hogs, two broad-tailed sheep, and a flock of Minorcan chickens, among other fauna, together with adequate fodder and grain. This makeshift barn/stable arrangement dislodged the crew; they were forced to move to the other quarters with their effects and hang their hammocks wherever they could find space. This sort of humiliating abuse of a United States warship was surely an official concern. Indeed, it was the straw that deservedly broke Captain Elliott's career. He was suspended from duty for four years, and never went to sea again.

After a brief overhaul at the Gosport Navy Yard in Virginia (now the Norfolk Navy Yard), *Constitution* was back to sea duty early in 1839, this time ordered to the Pacific as flagship under Commodore Alexander Claxton.

The ship sailed south in a leisurely fashion, stopping briefly in Cuba and Rio, and arriving in Valparaiso on South America's west coast in 87 days, having taken more than a week to clear Cape Horn. She moved up to the Peruvian coast, where she remained with very little to do, and returned home in October 1841.

At the end of her humdrum experience in the Pacific and along the west coast of South America, the venerable frigate had a further experience of little consequence in the Atlantic from 1842 to 1843. As flagship of the Home Squadron, *Constitution*, under Captain Foxhall Alexander, became an experimental gun platform for a new type of ordnance invented in France—shell-firing cannons with projectiles of 68 pounds each. After carpenters had spent considerable time making alterations to accommodate the oversize guns and ammunition, the frigate spent all of three weeks at sea testing the new guns. There is no record of these revolutionary cannons having been adopted.

In accordance with customary bureaucratic indecision and decision reversal, the gun-testing apparatus was placed aboard another ship, *Brandywine*, and *Constitution* was decommissioned in February 1843 in Norfolk, Virginia.

In early spring of the following year, at the behest of President John Tyler, who wished to activate this old and famous ship for diplomatic duty, the Norfolk command was ordered to recommission the now 47-year-old frigate. She was ready in April, but crew shortages delayed her departure until the end of May, when, under the command of Captain "Mad Jack" Percival, she departed with a full complement and orders to deliver the new American Minister to Brazil, and to proceed from there on a circumnavigation to show the flag. She sailed from west to east, from Rio de Janeiro around Cape of Good Hope to Mozambique and Madagascar. From there she sailed across the Indian Ocean to Southeast Asia. She put marines ashore in Muscat as a show of strength to the Sultan, and stopped at Turon Bay, now known as Da Nang, Vietnam, before continuing on to China, a newly opened continent, and anchoring in Macao. She then crossed the South Pacific, touching in the Philippines, Hawaii, and finally Monterey, Mexico. This voyage not only was an interesting experience for Captain Percival and his crew, but they were spreading as much goodwill as they were able while collecting flora and fauna from little-known places and people—accumulating geographic and economic knowledge. All of this contributed greatly to American foreign awareness and to the soon-to-begin Far East trade and the great Clipper Ship Era.

"Old Ironsides" finally turned back eastward, doubling Cape Horn, stopping again at Rio, completing the circuit and arriving at her home port of Boston in September 1846. For the old frigate, a layup was once again in order after such a long and what many thought would be her last voyage. She had sailed nearly 53,000 nautical miles around the planet, from west to east, against the prevailing trade winds. She had been in many climates and many seas, and had safely and routinely performed her duties. She was to be decommissioned for only two years, almost to the day.

In October 1848 she was fitted out and prepared for another tour as flagship in the Mediterranean. Wars and political instability again required her to carry an emissary to that region and preside over whatever seemed to be in the United States' interests. She headed directly into the Mediterranean, passing Gibraltar in a good time of 21 days, and continued on to Tripoli where she embarked the U.S. Consul for transfer to Egypt. She then returned to La Spezzia, Italy. While this was the currently assigned base for the American squadron, it was also at that time a loci of insurrection and expansionist goals. Elements of the Austrian army soon began a bombardment of Livorno, just south of La Spezzia, and the American ships began receiving and evacuating refugees. There were two other U.S. Navy ships there also: USS *Princeton* and the stores ship *Erie*.

This again brings to mind similar Mediterranean squadron activity that I personally experienced on board the American flagship USS *Raleigh* nearly 90 years later. In 1936–37 *Raleigh* was evacuating terror-stricken citizens, both American and Europeans, from the Spanish ports of Barcelona, Valencia, and Alicante during and after air bombardments by Francisco Franco's royalist forces. This continued for months. We were also spending considerable time on the Italian coast from Sicily to Genoa, both as a naval presence and diplomatic base, and participating in ceremonial activities. I can remember one morning in Naples when *Raleigh* fired 122 guns in salute to the crown prince for the birth of his son—as did *Constitution* in 1849 for the "accouchment of the Queen of Naples." In many ways, little changes in the Navy, even over centuries.

In September 1849, *Constitution*'s captain, John Gwinn, succumbed to a chronic illness while the ship was in Palermo, Sicily, where he had sought refuge ashore because of his ill health. This man, John Gwinn, was thoroughly hated by his crew. The records show that he had, during his time in command, ordered more corporal punishment than any other commanding officer; flogging occurred on the average of once a day, often for the slightest imagined offense. Captain Gwinn ruled a most unhappy ship, and upon his death, not surprisingly, there were celebrations by the crew—followed by more floggings ordered by Gwinn's relief, acting Captain Rowan, for misbehaving during the funeral.

Aside from short runs between Naples, Livorno, La Spezzia, and Genoa, and finally down the French coast to Toulon, France's naval center, *Constitution*'s further Mediterranean duties were without occasion. Before returning to the United States she transferred personnel in La Spezzia, took on stores, and finally hoisted her homeward-bound pennant on November 2, 1850. She left Gibraltar on December 1, once again ending a Mediterranean tour.

During this last cruise she had suffered two minor collisions to her by now much scarred and wounded hull. The second collision, with a British merchant brig, occurred shortly after leaving Gibraltar when she was homeward bound. In the dark, she struck the unlighted brig between the fore and main masts, and apparently rode right over the smaller vessel, for she left no floating evidence after the impact. The captain of the brig died, but the crew survived. These wet, bedraggled men had clung to the frigate's head and bowsprit rigging as she passed through their vessel, and they then pulled themselves aboard. One survivor clung to *Constitution*'s rudder for miles before his cries were heard.

Constitution arrived at the Brooklyn Navy Yard in New York on January 10, 1851, and was decommissioned again for just less than a year, when she was ordered once more to sail for the Eastern Atlantic and the Mediterranean. She did not actually depart until March 1853, as the new Commodore needed time to "settle in" to the flag officer's newly constructed quarters on the spar deck aft.

The *Constellation* problem

The period from 1851 until the Civil War was a very low period for the U.S. Navy. The old frigates like *Constitution*, *Constellation*, and *Congress* had outlived their combat usefulness, yet they hung on. The Navy had not been blessed by Congressional or Executive attention, and naval design and new construction were not matters on which to squander money—or even interest. Congress had ruled that there would be no new ships built; only money for repair and maintenance would be appropriated. Yet the older ships—the earlier "first" frigates—had deteriorated, most of them beyond use. *Constitution* had been fortunate, perhaps because of her reputation; she had obviously survived critical judgment in 1832 and had received necessary rejuvenation. But a prime example of the older ships was *Constellation*, the original of the first six—still afloat in 1853, but riddled with decay.

It is interesting to deviate from our protagonist ship briefly to discuss *Constellation*, if for no other reason than to support the assertion that there is but one surviving frigate. An old three-masted warship named *Constellation* now lies in Baltimore's Inner Harbor. Her sponsors identify her in their literature and promotion as the "U.S. frigate *Constellation*, the oldest warship." This is *not* a valid identity, for she is not the 36-gun frigate launched in Baltimore in 1797.

Recently there has been some renewed controversy on this mistaken identity. At the 1991 Naval History Symposium at the United States Naval Academy, an exhaustively researched paper was presented on the question of *Constellation*. Written by three scholarly researchers—Dana Wegner, Colan Ratliff, and Kevin Lynaugh of the David Taylor Research Center of the U.S. Navy—this 200-page book contains irrefutable documentation of the facts surrounding the disposition of the old U.S. frigate *Constellation* of 1797 and the U.S. sloop-of-war of the same name built in Norfolk in 1855. The book is published under the seal of the United States Navy, and is titled *Fouled Anchors: The* Constellation *Question Answered*.

A ship of larger dimensions than the old frigate and of basically different armament arrangement, sometimes called a corvette or a sloop-of-war, was built after the original *Constellation* had been scrapped in the same naval shipyard, the Gosport Navy Yard. She was given the same name as the earlier ship, as is and was the Navy's practice. This replacement was looked upon as an "administrative restoration."

The preservationists in the *Constellation* Historical Society, which maintains the 1855 relic, claim that the Navy has authenticated the old ship as the original *Constellation*. What they are apparently referring to is that some correspondence to that effect was signed by interim Navy officials who were also unaware of the facts, were being politically conciliatory, or both.

It requires but little research to discover *Constellation*'s official status. For example, the *List of Vessels of the United States Navy*, published in 1891 by the Government Printing Office, Washington, D.C., lists all the U.S. naval vessels of that time—their names, dimensions, where and when built, material, propulsion, rig, etc. Under "Sailing Vessels" there are twelve listed, one named *Constellation*—of 2,200 tons, built in 1854 at the Gosport Navy Yard. The year 1854 refers to the year the keel was laid, not the launching.

One further identifying characteristic provides evidence enough for anyone who understands the shipbuilding process: the placement of frames on the keel. The vessel now in Baltimore has frames separated by a common dimension that differs materially from those that Joshua Humphreys designed and were used in 1795–97. The contention made by the *Constellation* Historical Society at *Constellation*'s pier is that when the original vessel was "repaired and refitted in 1854," *they replaced the frames.* Any shipbuilder knows that in order to replace the frames, the entire hull's skeleton must be dismantled.[4] If this were the case then, with new frames of newly shaped geometry placed on a keel of greater length, the result is, by definition, a new and different ship. There is no argument about the "extant" *Constellation*, there is only a weak and biased defense of a cherished belief.

Last work for a sailing warship

Constitution's last voyage as an active warship in 1853–55 was directed primarily to the African coast, stopping to meet the Commodore of the Mediterranean squadron at La Spezzia for a command change. When the old frigate finally arrived on the Italian coast, her new flag officer was Commodore Isaac Mayo, who had been aboard since sailing from New York. Mayo, apparently in no hurry to take over his new duties, passed leisurely through the Mediterranean from Gibraltar, where he had lain five days after arriving. After relieving the homebound Squadron Commodore in La Spezzia, Mayo proceeded on a sightseeing tour of the Italian region and on to the southern coast, calling at Tunis, Algiers, and Tangier, not returning to Gibraltar until early June. He had left New York on March 2, and his primary duties were to patrol the African Atlantic coast to enforce the laws prohibiting the transport of slaves.

Constitution finally arrived in August on or near the African coast, where her patrol began, out of Monrovia. On this patrol Commodore Mayo successfully played a useful part in fighting the slave trade. Together with U.S. Marines and sailors he subdued a tribal chieftan who raided neighboring tribes to capture slaves, selling them at the beachhead slave market.

A month later *Constitution* intercepted a slaver, the American schooner *Gambril*, took her and the crew as a prize and, under command of a lieutenant from *Constitution*, sent her back to the United States for disposition.

The old frigate remained cruising in the broad, undefined station, calling at ports as far south as the lonely island of St. Helena—Napoleon's final exile. For nearly six months she cruised and paid calls at Monrovia, the Cape Verde Islands, and the equatorial coast. There is record of another collision, with little damage, in which *Constitution* was struck or accidentally rammed by an American whaling bark in Porto Praya, on the coast of Senegal.

Constitution returned home after two-and-a-quarter years, arriving, by

Figure 3-1. This very early photograph shows the old frigate hauled completely out of water beyond a drydock in Portsmouth, New Hampshire. There were not many drydocks in 1858, and these were busy with more modern and active naval vessels. It is most interesting to see *Constitution* here with a figurehead, the second and more expert carving of President Andrew Jackson.

way of the Caribbean, at the Portsmouth Navy Yard, New Hampshire, in early June 1855.

Constitution's cruise to Africa marks the end of her active career as a warship. The Navy was now gradually mechanizing frigate-type ships with auxiliary steam power. The old, traditional sailing ships, which kept to the winds' schedules and had to be towed in and out of harbors by steam tugs, were no longer considered dependable for modern warfare.

Sailing warships were assuming their humble place as second-class ships or less—and the Civil War was to accelerate their decline. Shipbuilding technology was nearing the days of iron and steel. Although in 1855 the men who comprised the U.S. naval establishment could not know that in just six more years a ridiculous-looking metal contraption—scorned as a "cheese box" on a raft—fabricated in Greenpoint, Long Island, New York, would change the manner of naval warfare universally. The *Monitor*'s successful operation made a knowledgeable historian say, "Probably no naval conflict in the history of the world ever attracted so much attention as did the Battle of Hampton Roads, between the *Monitor* and the *Merrimac*."[5] The *London Times*, in March 1862, made the sad observation, "Whereas we [the British] had available for immediate purposes, 149 first class warships—there is not now a ship in the English Navy, apart from two new ironclads, that it would not be madness to trust in an engagement with that little *Monitor*."

A school ship for midshipmen

With the establishment of the U.S. Naval Academy at Annapolis in 1849, it soon became apparent that, during their four-year academic pursuit, the midshipmen also needed some sort of shipboard experience. So, in 1858, USS *Constitution* was withdrawn from her soggy ordinary in the bogs at the Portsmouth Navy Yard and headed for another restoration. This time the historic frigate, now 60 years old, was to become a school ship.

She was fitted inside for study rooms and living quarters, with lockers and washbasins, and recommissioned as a school ship on August 1, 1860. Commanded by David Dixon Porter, then a lieutenant, she weighed anchor for Annapolis for her first recorded visit since she left to join the War of 1812. About ten days later, this now second-class ship embarked her first shorebound midshipmen—130 "plebes", fourth-class midshipmen in their first year of study. The superintendent deemed it wise to separate these confused young men from the influence of upperclassmen, and at the same time introduce them to life at sea.

The midshipmen were not long aboard their new school ship before the clouds of war spied months before Abraham Lincoln took his oath of office in March 1861 began to gather in earnest. From the Severn River in Annapolis where "Old Ironsides" was lying, her cargo of starry-eyed young aspirants to the naval life could clearly see on the opposite shore young, gray-clad militiamen training—Southern sympathizers, as were most of the citizens of Maryland. The Commandant at the Naval Academy closed the gates and ordered a doubling of security, alerting the Marine contingent to guard against any possible anti-Union raid. The railroad north through Baltimore was closed to through traffic. The feeling of paranoia grew, and after Lincoln's election conflicts and protests erupted in the streets of Baltimore and Annapolis against any significant shows of loyalty toward the Union and to the United States.

As matters deteriorated and evacuations were ordered in other threatened U.S. military commands, such as Pensacola and Norfolk, it was decided that the Naval Academy would be better situated in a "solid Northern" state. On April 25, 1861, *Constitution* left the Navy guns at the old fort on the Severn and was finally underway with Union midshipmen as well as faculty and materiel for the naval school. After some difficulty with the shoal water—she was ignominiously towed down the Chesapeake Bay in company with the steam vessel *Harriet Lane*—*Constitution* cleared the Capes for New York and the naval academy's new home, in Newport, Rhode Island.

The American Civil War was not a war for the old frigate *Constitution*. She was 65 years old, well past a ship's retirement age, but also explicitly of an obsolete style. The most significant naval engagement of this war between the states was that between the USS *Monitor* and the Confederate States' CSS *Virginia* (formerly the USS *Merrimac*). The battle itself was inconclusive, but it was tremendously significant in prompting the U.S. to close the book forever on future wooden warships. It meant the end even of steam-powered wooden war vessels, as predicted by leading naval thinkers in Great Britain. However, it took some time and technology to convert to ironclads.

The most decisive naval conflict involving ironclads took place on the Mississippi when Admiral Farragut's iron ships silenced the forts protecting Vicksburg. Farragut's victory at Mobile Bay further proved the usefulness of iron warships.

Constitution returned to Annapolis in 1865 at the close of the Civil War to continue her career as a training and school ship. Other sailing warships such as *Macedonian* (frigate, built 1832), *John Adams* (ship sloop-of-war, built 1830), and *Constellation* (corvette, built 1855) were sail training ships, but "Old Ironsides" remained at the wharf—humble pie indeed for the old warrior. Now converted for classrooms and quarters for midshipmen, with a roofed-over waist amidships, *Constitution* was no longer in sailing shape . . . and her condition continued to deteriorate until in the summer of 1871 it became necessary for her to retire. She was towed to the Philadelphia Navy Yard that September. Repair and restoration work did not begin—other than the dismantling of her rig—for about two years. In the usual bureaucratic shuffle, no money had been authorized, and no consensus about her fate. Scrap her or preserve her? She was becoming a very white elephant—an albatross to hang about the neck of anyone who said, "Don't scrap her!" The Navy had emerged from the Civil War with almost 700 commissioned warships, yet a decade later the fleet had dwindled to near 50 outmoded vessels, as America once again forgot the importance of the sea and sea power. The vestigial navy—ranked behind even Denmark and Chile in naval power—had no role for a tired old ship like *Constitution*, and no money for her repairs.

Centennial restoration, 1873–76

Even in her most dire straits, some saving situation always seems to emerge for "Old Ironsides." Early in 1873 it occurred to some authority with sense for history and a compelling sympathy for preservation that the country's Centennial was but three years off, and preserving this link with the country's beginnings, as a historic exhibit open to the public, would be a grand project. Considering the old frigate's deteriorating condition, it would probably take three years to restore her.

The restoration work proceeded more slowly than anticipated because, among other things, the Philadelphia Navy Yard was being moved, ship

Figure 3-2. This lithograph shows *Constitution* underway in the latter half of the 19th century, probably between the end of the Civil War and 1871. Sailing well under topsails and fore course, she is in company with a steam frigate, USS *Kearsarge*, famous for her Civil War battle with CSS *Alabama*, and an unidentified sloop-of-war in the background, possibly *Constellation*.

by ship, to a new location. In the process, *Constitution* became one of the last ships remaining in the old yard. She was first stripped of her planking to the waterline, followed by the replacement of deteriorated wood. Figures 3-3 and 3-4 show the stripped hull with a nearly solid wall of exposed frames. Looking closely at these photographs, one can see the extended plank fastenings in places where the planks were ripped off.

It was during this restoration, 1873–76, that many changes were made in her appearance—perhaps more than in any other overhaul. With no consistent record of all the changes, large and small, we can at present only study the results and account for where and when a very few of them took place. The figure of Andrew Jackson beheaded in Boston in 1834 had, in interim years, been replaced with a more expertly carved figure by Isaac

Fowle, a protégé of figurehead designer William Rush. But it was still a political figure, out of place on the bow of a U.S. naval ship. It was here, in the Philadelphia yard in 1874, that this second Andrew Jackson figurehead was removed—and if a ship could express relief, her venerable timbers must have relaxed after that painless extraction. In its place was inset a carved scroll head similar to the one that exists today.

The progression of various decorations on the extremity of *Constitution*'s stemhead—first the Hercules figure, then the Maltese billethead followed by Train's artful replacement, the controversial Jackson statue and its replacement, and finally a scroll head—are an interesting study that could be a matter of deep research. It is a pity that *Constitution* was not more lastingly graced by the work of early Federal figurehead artists like John Skillin, who carved her original figurehead (described in Chapter Two). Skillin was one of the first American carvers to discard the English tradition of elaborate detail. He worked from William Rush's designs, which showed the strong influence of the great French sculptor Houdon, under whom Rush studied. One of Rush's finest examples of ship figures is that of Benjamin Franklin, carved for the U.S. 74-gun ship-of-the-line *Franklin* in 1815; this figure is now in the United States Naval Academy Museum.

Sadly, *Constitution*'s fortunes never allowed her to have a fine and appropriate carving for her stemhead—other than perhaps the original, so early lost. During her active career, the replacement of a fine figurehead was, understandably, of small priority—and during her later restorations there was no one able to do the appropriate work. The empty stemhead of the stripped-down hull in the Figure 3-3 photograph of 1874 looks bleakly naked indeed.

After emerging from her lengthy overhaul and restoration in late 1876, too late for any serious participation in the National Centennial ceremonies, "Old Ironsides" remained at her berth in Philadelphia—still something of an enigma for the naval establishment.

For a while she continued to serve as a school ship for apprentices and new enlistees, until early 1878 when she was refitted for a special assign-

Figure 3-3. In 1873, *Constitution* had been retired to the Philadelphia Navy Yard for an extensive restoration. She was finally hauled out on building ways in March 1874. This illustration is from an original photograph showing her stripped of planking from her upper deck rail to her waterline. Close examination of the picture shows her copper sheathing still in place, with flotation lines marking the various levels of harbor stains; this raises the question of whether her planking was completely removed, as some records indicate.

ment: to carry American exhibits to the 1878 World Exposition in France. Departing in February, she encountered gales and heavy seas typical for the season. In fact, the entire cruise to Le Havre and back with her special cargo was visited by gales, groundings, collision, and problems with foreign authorities.

On her return in January 1879 she grounded on the south coast of England, and a diplomatic squabble ensued about the salvage payments to the various tugs and lighters needed for her "rescue." She was docked in Portsmouth, England, for appraisal of the damage; the keel shoe was

Figure 3-4. This 1874 photograph of *Constitution* docking, during the same haulout as in Figure 3-3, shows the stern view of the ship. The planking has been removed above the waterline and down to the upturn of the stern quarters at the after end. The rudder has been removed for repair or replacement.

repaired and some copper sheets were replaced. Continuing her ill-starred voyage through heavy seas and gales in the Bay of Biscay, she lost her rudder, rigged a jury rudder, and put into Lisbon for dockyard rudder replacement. A word must be said for her captain on this unhappy voyage: Oscar C. Badger exhibited exemplary seamanship and command—especially in bringing a rudderless ship to port. I am certain that Captain Badger passed on this remarkable naval expertise to his grandson, Admiral Oscar C. Badger II, who became a wartime hero in World War II, and under whom I had the privilege of serving.

After her mission to France, *Constitution* continued on as a training ship for apprentices, cruising between the Caribbean and Nova Scotia. At the end of 1880 she returned to Philadelphia for another overhaul and assessment of her condition. After a thorough recaulking, refitting of her rudder, and the drilling of test borings, she was considered in fit enough condition to return to duty, such as it was, in April 1881.

Restoring an historic property, 1907–08 and 1927–30

Essentially, at the turn of the century, *Constitution*'s active career was coming to an end. The Navy was in a fiscal swamp, with no money for new ships, or repair or maintenance of old ships. The old wooden frigate, a relic of another era, was retired to the Portsmouth Navy Yard, outfitted with an ugly barn-like building covering her spar deck, and given the only title that held an ounce of dignity: the "Receiving Ship," a term for ships perhaps one voyage away from complete obsolescence.

This retirement and accompanying deterioration continued until Congress, at the behest of Boston Congressman John F. Fitzgerald, prevailed to have her towed to Boston, with adequate repair, to celebrate her 100th birthday.

She was returned to Boston in time for her own centennial, but there was much to be done. By the turn of the 20th century *Constitution* was becoming a political issue. Under pressure from the people of Boston, Congress authorized her repair and restoration, but without appropriating any funds. This has long been a nice political ploy, giving the appearance of acting without actually having to do so, but it is only briefly satisfying. (This same situation existed in 1992; Congress had authorized a restoration of the *Constitution*, but without the financial support necessary to carry it out.) The Massachusetts United Daughters of the War of 1812 began a campaign to raise $400,000 for the restoration. Unhappily, no more than a few hundred dollars were forthcoming.

In 1903 the Historical Societies of Boston and New England petitioned

Figure 3-5. *Constitution* undergoing repair on Drydock No. 1, Charlestown Navy Yard, Boston, 1927; view looking aft from the bow.

Congress for monies to restore the ship, calling it the "Fighting Frigate of 1812." Charles Francis Adams—the President of the Historical Society, the descendant of presidents, and yet to be Secretary of the Navy—was first to sign the petition. This apparently made no great impression on Congress or the administration, for in 1905 the Secretary of the Navy under President Theodore Roosevelt proposed in an annual report that the frigate *Constitution*, being "old and no longer useful," be made a target for the North Atlantic Fleet to use for gunnery practice, and to be "sunk by their fire." This sort of talk was enough to arouse a popular outcry and to cause the Secretary to be transferred to a new job as Postmaster General.

A Picture Portfolio by
WILLIAM GILKERSON

USS *Constitution*
in 1812, hove-to for
target practice. Artist's note:
"Old Ironsides" was variously rigged
and painted at different times throughout her
career; this drawing follows the only contemporary model of the ship, the model presented to
Isaac Hull by his crew after the defeat of HMS *Guerriere* in 1812 and today displayed at the
Peabody Museum of Salem, Massachusetts.

OLD IRONSIDES

OLD IRONSIDES

A make-and-mend Sunday aboard *Constitution*: A boatswain supervises a young seaman roving a replacement carronade training tackle as a marine looks on and the captain, in full-dress uniform, observes his quarterdeck. Originally, the ship's spar-deck bulwarks terminated at the caprail over the carronade ports, and the hammock nettings were situated as shown; as the ship is today, her bulwarks have been built higher and her nettings have been raised.

USS *Constitution* firing a signal gun, 1812.

OLD IRONSIDES

OLD IRONSIDES

OLD IRONSIDES

Constitution pursued by two British frigates, HMS *Junon* and HMS *Tenedos*, off Cape Ann, Massachusetts, April 3, 1814. With the aid of every sail she could carry (including royal studding sails), "Old Ironsides" evaded her powerful opponents, taking temporary refuge in Gloucester Harbor.

(Courtesy of the U.S. Naval Academy Museum, the Beverley R. Robinson Collection.)

(Preceding pages) Near the Canary Islands on the moonlit night of February 20, 1815, *Constitution* encountered HMS *Levant*, 21 guns, and HMS *Cyane*, 34 guns, and commenced firing with all ships running before the light breeze; initially the smaller British warships were in line, with the American frigate to their starboard. In the gathering smoke, *Cyane* attempted to turn across *Constitution*'s stern, but the American captain, Stuart, turned to port, braked by backing her main and mizzen topsails, and continued the engagement to both sides. *Levant*, badly shot up, was forced to run downwind until she could effect repairs, while *Constitution* concentrated her fire on *Cyane* with artillery and—moments later—rifle, musket, and swivel fire from the fighting tops.

The biggest of *Constitution*'s fighting tops was the livingroom-size maintop (left), a 21-foot by 16-foot platform (at the bottom of the 20-foot-high doubling) easily accommodating its 18- to 20-man crew of topmen and marines.

(Courtesy of the USS *Constitution* Museum, Boston.)

Constitution raking H.M. frigate *Java*, December 29, 1812, off the coast of Brazil. Having attempted to come about, *Java* is caught in irons, allowing *Constitution* to cross her stern.
(Courtesy of the U.S. Naval Academy Museum, the Beverley R. Robinson Collection.)

OLD IRONSIDES

Figure 3-6. During the same repair as in Figure 3-5; stern view.

Finally, 1906 saw a Naval Appropriations Act with a provision of money to repair *Constitution*. Naval constructor Rear Admiral Elliott Snow was put in charge of the work.

The restoration in 1907–08 was restricted to the funds available. The ship was not drydocked; hence, it was impossible to make underwater repair, examine critical timbers or planking, or renew her copper. The work, almost totally confined to the restoration of the topsides, new spars and rigging, was essentially a cosmetic refinish, a facelift intended to disguise and postpone any serious repair. But the total bill for the job fit the Congressional appropriation of $100,000. "Old Ironsides" was thenceforth to become a patriotic exhibit at the Navy yard in Boston.

Tour guides led visitors through the ship, while she slowly settled into decay, until Admiral Eberle, the Chief of Naval Operations, ordered the Board of Inspection and Survey to conduct a complete material survey with recommendations; this was accomplished in early 1924. The results of this survey exposed a shocking condition of a ship full of decay and distortion. Again, Congress was asked for an appropriation for a complete restoration, and politics took its usual stance. Congress readily authorized the restoration, but agreed with the Secretary of the Navy's suggestion that the money should be solicited from the citizens of the country. What the Secretary's motivations were we cannot know, but Congress would rejoice and remember not having to appropriate money—in this case, something like three-quarters of a million dollars.

The authorization actually began in March 1925, and this time it was understood to be a restoration of the highest magnitude. The Navy's initial efforts began slowly and within the scope of the regular "in-house" operations: research on existing plans of the ship, which turned up very little, and the determination of material requirements and availability of wood species, etc.

The public funding effort was slow, too, at first, but it gradually took hold in a nationwide display of support. The campaign, begun initially by schoolchildren, was sufficiently successful to sustain momentum. Things were helped along by a Hollywood production called "Old Ironsides" (of course), with a star-studded cast that included Wallace Berry, Esther Ralston, and George Bancroft. The filmmakers even went as far as to build a full-scale replica of *Constitution*, which was more of a mock-up conversion of the Maine-built ship *Llewellyn J. Morse*. After the filming, the replica was deliberately destroyed. Whatever money the film returned in box-office receipts was not nearly as important as its raising of public awareness.

In the meantime, Lieutenant John Lord, a Naval Constructor, was put in charge of the restoration, and the Secretary of the Navy gave official direction that it should proceed in April 1927. As the old ship was dismantled, some of the unsalvageable material—such as copper nails, bits of wood, rope, etc.—became souvenirs used in the fund-raising campaign.

As a schoolboy I invested $5 in a little chip of wood with an identification sticker on it from "Old Ironsides."

The old frigate was stripped of her rigging, spars, and masts by early May 1927 and made ready for drying out. Her gun batteries and interior furnishings were removed. The ship was shored inside, and she was specially braced both internally as well as externally (Figure 3-5) to distribute the docking forces after she was no longer supported by the more gentle, buoyant water. Additional ballast was added amidships to provide greater downward force to the anti-hog equation. In fact, the ship's distortion was more severe than at first believed. It was probably not much more distorted than 20 years before, but it was now, at long last, being looked at by a more educated naval engineer.

At this point, I will not detail the various engineering approaches to that drydocking and the subsequent restoration. Much of this theory and practice will be covered in the next chapter, in reviewing the most recent (1991) structural assessment and recommendations for improving her present condition today.

The restoration work of 1927–30 was the most extensive that *Constitution* had ever had—and none too soon. It perhaps could have been more extensive, however, and with some of the technology and preservation measures available today, the ship would likely be in better shape now.

Lieutenant Lord recognized that the distortion existed in three dimensions. She not only was hogged longitudinally, but she was unsymmetrical, being about 11½ inches wider to port than to starboard. There is no record of her bilges having sagged, but one can make a fairly good presumption of that, judging by the hogging, which was recorded to be in the magnitude of about 14½ inches amidships.

After the ship had been carefully docked in a crib-like structure, the structural restoration took place in a very thorough manner. The interior bottom ceiling was in very bad condition and was largely removed as far up as the berth deck for replacement. The frame futtocks were examined, and many were badly decayed. This deterioration was random, and rotten

Figure 3-7. The restored ship is undocked. In this extensive restoration of 1927–30, she was strengthened by restoring timbers, sister keelsons, decks, ceiling, and planking, and freshly painted. After undocking she would be re-rigged, recommissioned, and sent on a nationwide cruise, visiting East and West Coast seaports.

sections were replaced as high as the third or fourth futtock. The breast-hooks forward below the waterline level were decayed and replaced. The keel was found to be in good condition, but the keelson was decayed and fractured; not only was it replaced, but sister keelsons were fitted on both sides to improve longitudinal strength. The framing forward of the transom in the tuck of the stern was rejuvenated.

After the structural frame had been restored, the inner ceiling was replaced. Originally it had been longleaf or Southern pine, a wood that historically has had extensive use in wooden ships, but this time Douglas-fir was used, since longleaf yellow pine was unavailable. Much new exterior planking was needed, especially above the waterline, and it was of white oak.

According to the official Navy report from the district commandant upon the completion of the restoration, there were no main wales, middle wales, or upper wales along the topside planking before the work began. These wales, longitudinal heavy planking strakes of almost double thickness, were specified by Joshua Humphreys in the original construction. There is, of course, no record as to when they were removed and not replaced. The wales were included in this 1927–30 restoration and surely brought back considerable longitudinal strength.

Figure 3-8. The old frigate at 134 years, afloat—after nearly five years of intensive reconstruction and re-rigging. This 1931 photo taken in Boston Harbor shows her ready, here at the end of a towline, to begin her nationwide cruise.

Constitution was out of drydock in mid-March 1930, and in the autumn of that year was ready for service. At the time, she had not been recommissioned for duty, but the new Secretary of the Navy, Charles Francis Adams, being from Boston and of the Historical Society, had plans for the newly reconditioned ship.

Nationwide cruise, 1931

After *Constitution* was recommissioned, Secretary of the Navy Charles Francis Adams announced that "Old Ironsides" would make a nationwide cruise, visiting seaports on both the Atlantic and Pacific coasts in a tour of gratitude for the public who had contributed so generously to her restoration. In her reconditioned splendor, the 134-year-old frigate was towed by a Navy sea-going tug around the entire coastal United States and its freshwater tributaries. It may have been more impressive if *Constitution* had sailed the coast, but at the time there were no sailing ship sailors in the Navy and it would have taken several years to train enough of a crew for such a cruise. When in port, however, the tug discreetly found a place to be less visible.

The frigate's captain on this cruise was Commander Louis J. Gulliver. I remember his name particularly and with some sadness, not because I knew Captain Gulliver personally, but I knew his son very well. We were shipmates and close friends for several memorable years. "Louie" was detached from our ship and sent out to China and the Asiatic squadron. He was lost with his ship, a river gunboat built for the U.S. patrol on the Yangtze River, somewhere in the South China Sea. The last message from this gallant little vessel in 1942 was, "—sighted Japanese cruisers—preparing to attack them."

A further note about Louis J. Gulliver, Jr., and an interesting statistic, is that he was the last regular U.S. Navy midshipman to serve on the USS *Constitution* at sea. While he was a third-classman at the Naval Academy, he gave up his summer cruise and annual leave to accompany *Constitution* on this national cruise. Probably, also, his experience was singular in that as a midshipman he served under his father, the commanding officer on the frigate. He told me that it was no vacation cruise; he was part of the officer contingent and stood regular watches.

This East Coast–West Coast exposure would bring *Constitution* much popular acclamation, the most in her entire career. She had been saved several times over the years by public generosity; most of her previous benefactors were never to see her. During this 22,000-mile goodwill voyage, lasting from 1931 to 1934, over four-and-a-half million Americans would come to see her and walk her decks.

It was on this cruise that I had the exciting experience of boarding her as a midshipman, along with a number of my classmates, as she visited Annapolis by special invitation. We were permitted below as well as aloft, to a limited height, to the fore and main tops. It is a good memory still.

4

The State of the Surviving Frigate

We have brought this old frigate's history along from her birth at the end of the 18th century to her 20th-century overhaul of 1927–30, when as a very old and tired ship she received her greatest restoration. In this chapter we will study her present condition, and in the next we will discuss how this national monument might be preserved into the 21st century.

When she returned to Boston in 1934 after her triumphant nationwide cruise, "Old Ironsides" entered her old berth at the former Charlestown Navy Yard, where she has resided ever since, an historic relic in a city of historic relics (Figure 4-1), and an officially commissioned vessel of the United States Navy, with a commanding officer and crew—fully rigged and proudly flying her commission pennant and the national ensign at her peak. The crew, in historic 1812 uniform, politely and professionally escort the thousands of visitors about the ship daily. She also has a watchful maintenance group nearby in the old Navy yard facilities under the direction of Donald Turner, head of *Constitution*'s Maintenance and Repair Division.

Figure 4-1. After returning to Boston from her 35-month cruise, "Old Ironsides" was tied alongside Pier No. 1 West as an historic exhibit.

To the untrained eye, she looks beautiful—a well-preserved relic of a bygone age. But how well-preserved is she? *Constitution* was drydocked for inspection and maintenance in 1936, 1945, 1957, and 1973–74, but it has now been 18 years since her old hull below the waterline has seen the light of day or had its copper sheathing restored. As time goes on and this proud old symbol of our country's beginnings approaches her bicentennial year, she has not been rewarded with an accelerated drydocking schedule for necessary maintenance; rather, they have become more and more widely separated.

For those charged with her adequate maintenance, this is worrisome. The hogging along her keel is not a new thing; I have mentioned earlier that hogging is a common condition, even soon after launching, of which shipbuilders are well aware. Keel hogging cannot easily be prevented or easily rectified once begun. In older ships, greater keel deflection is inevitable, and the dimensions usually become more extreme with aging. Hogging is also symptomatic of distortion in the bottom, sides, and decks.

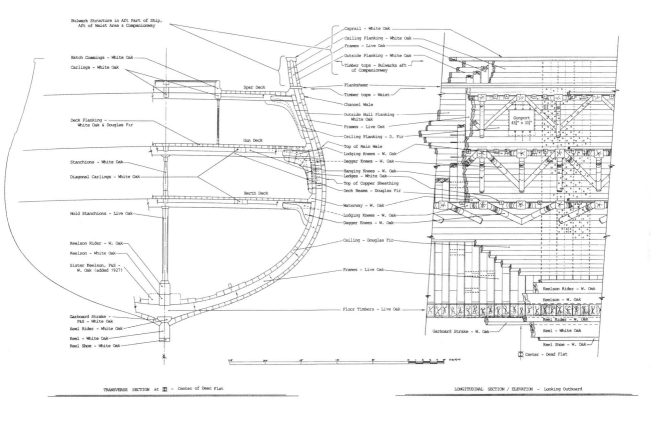

Figure 4-2. The structural sections of the old frigate provide helpful information for assessing her strengths and weaknesses. The view on the left is a projection of her mid-section showing the transverse members and the species of woods used. On the right is a section near amidships projecting longitudinally the structural parts including the ceiling, frames, and planking from the keel shoe up to the caprail. This drawing has been constructed to show the components in place following the extensive overhaul of 1927–30.

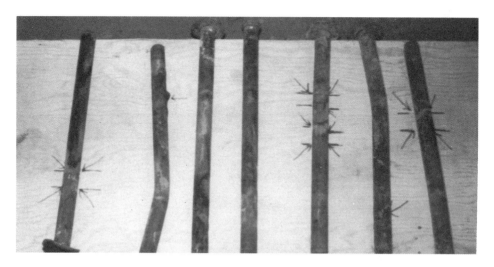

Figure 4-3. Specimen copper fastenings withdrawn from planking and frames; the arrows on the plywood indicate locations of mild erosion. Approximately 17 inches long, these essentially cylindrical fastenings were forged flat toward the ends and left blunt.

This hull distortion—a general flaw in the ship's fore-and-aft symmetry—exists in *Constitution* today. We do not know its exact distribution, but we can be sure that it is increasing—at an unknown rate. Her beam, when last measured, indicates that she is more than 1 foot wider than originally designed; the keel amidships was hogged nearly 15 inches above a straight line between similar points at its juncture with stern and stem. We can be sure that her bilges have sagged outward and her decks have moved accordingly, and that her starboard hull shape does not match her port side.

But these things, plus the extent of hidden decay, are altogether no reason for despair. "Old Ironsides" has spent more of her life rocking along in some such alarming condition than she has spent in the robust health of her fighting days. But just because she is not and never will be like new again is no reason to abandon her—as has been suggested by some, and feared by others.

There is a brighter side. *Constitution* was and is a strong ship. She has a core between her inner and outer skins of live oak—a very strong, decay-resistant wood. Her sides and bottom are of another fine species, with proven longitudinal strength—American white oak, the "iron sides" that in her youth deflected cannonballs. Her inner planking (ceiling) is a more resilient and flexible American wood, Douglas-fir. These more important outer and inner surface woods are easy to inspect and some have been replaced as needed. Her fastenings have been recently tested from the inside and are generally in good condition.

Having said this much, I will add only that at present we cannot take our eyes off the ultimate target: restoration that will ensure her continued survival. This is not the time for apathy and procrastination. If we take that course, our ship will fall into a state of decay and disrepair from which there will be no return—and that could happen sooner than later.

Structural assessment

In March 1991 I was asked by the Surface Ship's Structural Integrity Division of the Navy to personally conduct a structural assessment of *Constitution*, and make recommendations for correcting inadequate hull strength and distortion and restoring the ship both structurally and aesthetically—for me a challenging directive, and one I approached humbly.

Let us begin by looking at the core of the structural assessment, for I believe it provides a unique base for a discussion of the ship's current condition as well as a guide to the analysis and proposals that concern *Constitution*'s future.

Before my involvement, a number of reports were prepared or contracted for by various government agencies in response to requests for specific advice and/or proposals as to the extent of *Constitution*'s problems. Here is a list of some of the more significant ones:

- "Recommendations for the FY (fiscal year) 1992 Drydocking Restricted Availability of USS *Constitution*," NAVSEA Report No. 803-6516802.

- "USS *Constitution* Model Test Results of a 16:1 Scale Wooden Model and a 16:1 Scale Model Composite Space Frame," NAVSEA Report 803-6517024.

- "Longitudinal Strength Data—SHCP Output and Section Properties for Station 10."

- Survey critiques by: Rick Farris, Inc., Marine Surveyors; fastenings examination.
  Portsmouth Naval Shipyard; plank fastenings tests.

- Forest Products Laboratory Study, Department of Agriculture; laboratory study (testing of wood samples for strength).

All of the people involved in these earlier assessments are experts in their fields, and have devoted time both to study *Constitution*'s current health and to offer some methods of strengthening any perceived weaknesses. Part of my directive was to study these reports, find what was in my opinion useful or applicable in the restoration of the venerable *Constitution*—in the event that the Navy should undertake such a project.

"No unapproved deviations"

I began my own assessment by looking into the origin of the *Constitution*'s design, which I believe establishes an essential baseline of authenticity from which to proceed. There must be a correct graphic image of the original ship, viable specifications that will substantively resist challenge from historians and experts. As a naval architect I am concerned with the shape, structure, and correct image of the ship, so to begin with I was most interested in an authentic profile—the lines configuration of the hull.

Some people ask: How do you know she was built according to the design and to her designer's intent? Can we believe that the plans were followed correctly? Did the builder have authority to make changes in the plans, either major or minor? These are, of course, legitimate questions. But I think the answers to them are quite clear. Research proves that the plans and drawings approved by Joshua Humphreys are original. Research also proves that these plans were correctly executed.

Delving into the tomes of correspondence between designers, draftsmen, Congressmen, the Secretaries of the Navy and of War, and shipbuilders of 1795–97 is an arduous task. But much of it has been done for us by William Bass in a recent *Naval History* article[1] and by Messrs. Wegner, Ratliff, and Lynaugh in the Navy's Taylor Research Center publication of their recent study of the authenticity of USS *Constellation*. In the latter work, we get a clear indication that the builders were faithful to Humphreys's design, even if there were several ships being built simultaneously and Humphreys had to trust the naval agents to see his designs carried out. The builders, Wegner and company write in their book, *Fouled Anchors: The Constellation Question Answered* (U.S. Navy, 1991), ". . . have acted as naval agents. Humphreys's final plans were drafted by William Doughty, Clerk of Humphreys's Yard in Philadelphia, and completed on January 15, 1795. Following lofting, molds were prepared and drawings were shipped in a tin case from Philadelphia to the naval agent. . . ."

"In no uncertain terms," they continue, "all superintendents, constructors, and agents were initially ordered, then repeatedly reminded, that there were to be no unapproved deviations from the master plans and specifications."

Joshua Humphreys was a responsible contractor, and I believe that *Constitution*, like her sisterships, began her life according to Humphreys's specifications and his lines as drafted by William Doughty. I think the new ship appeared much like the reconstructed profile in Figure 2-12, described in Chapter Two.

This said, in the building of a complex structure like *Constitution*, we may well ask whether the plans really were followed in every detail, despite dire warnings. In particular, we now question whether there was an omission—approved or not—concerning the diagonal riders over the frames and inner ceiling of the bottom below the berth deck. In Humphreys's alleged specifications (of which there is no original), these diagonal riders were to be installed six per side forward and aft of the midsection. Captain Tyrone Martin, former commanding officer of *Constitution* and a most diligent scholar of the ship's history, thinks that the riders were installed. This may be based, but it is doubtful, on a rather weak inference in the 1927 overhaul plans of Lieutenant Lord that say that Humphreys's "risers" would be replaced. If they were installed, one wonders when they were removed, for there is no evidence of the riders today, nor of their removal.

It is also quite believable that they were never installed. These diagonal riders would, in the normal construction sequence, be the last of the hull's structural timbers to go in, just before the decking. It is quite possible that in the press of completing the ship, already overdue, they were left out. Perhaps Humphreys agreed to leave them out, if he ever specified them; frigates were generally built without such complex and difficult-to-install spiral-like diagonals made of heavy scantling timber. So it is believable, too, that Humphreys gave verbal permission that they be omitted. Nothing of this was recorded—nor is there evidence in the records of other American frigates of a similar structure. Yet it would have been very good had these diagonal riders been part of *Constitution*'s structure, for they may have proved a preventive against hogging—that is their purpose. They were standard in British ships of 74 guns and larger. *Constitution* was nearly as large.

Figure 4-2, a drawing of the transverse section and middle body sectional elevation, shows the authentic structure, much as the ship was built and much as it exists today, with noted additions.

Gathering information

Since it was my job to comment upon government-furnished studies of *Constitution*'s structural integrity, I began by reviewing the ship's record of maintenance. The first document I studied was one titled "Ship's Maintenance Manual," a most helpful reference source prepared by Naval Architect P. W. Witherell. A high percentage of it is not applicable to the problems involved in the study for the assessment of *Constitution*, but there are other items that are useful.

In particular, I did not agree with Witherell's recommended reinforcement after keel straightening. In my report, I wrote:

It is of course correct to recognize that some of the hogging is built into the ship's form through the various replanking of sides and deck and that this should be removed to assist the hull in relaxing toward its proper form. However, the means recommended to restrain the hull from resuming distortion are, I feel, inappropriate. The addition of steel box girders replacing sister keelsons and a continuous steel band wrapped around the entire ship's upper hull will add to the problems rather than correct them. I believe that there are more traditional approaches to the problem and that the ship's normal strength girder characteristics must not be ignored.

The second document I studied, "Recommendations for Drydocking (DRAV)," is most interesting and extensive, but, again, one with which I cannot wholly agree. I wrote:

The first paragraph on diagonal riders I find unsupported. This paragraph states that both the 1834 building specifications for a 44-gun frigate and the drawings indicate the ship originally had six pairs of $9'' \times 16''$ diagonal riders. It is understandable that 1834 building specifications for a warship of the *Constitution*'s size may have called for diagonal riders. The referenced drawing is the midship section structure of the vessel as before the 1927 restoration, drawn and dated "February 1926." It implies that previously existing diagonal "riders" will be incorporated in the restoration or it may be so understood in the wording in the drawing's legend. Whatever the intention, there were no riders, either transverse or diagonal, apparently installed during the 1927–30 restoration. There is no indication at this time that such members were a part of the original structure.

On the other hand, I agree with the report's recommendation that such diagonal riders should be considered in any future restoration. While I further agree that a longitudinal stiffener or reinforced keel/keelson assembly will do little to arrest the "continuing hull deflection," it is my strong belief that the "deflection" which is continually referred to in a "longitudinal" orientation, or "keel" deflection and hog, is a symptom of the overall distortion problem.

Before going further with my comments on the government-furnished documents, I should describe the infrastructure of concerned Navy offices and agencies that have submitted these suggestions on *Constitution*'s behalf. First, the ship is in the old Charlestown Navy Yard in Boston, which, of course, is no longer a regular Navy yard. However, the frigate is in commission there, under the watchful eye of the Naval Historical Center Detachment Boston, USS *Constitution* Maintenance and Repair Facility. This agency, the immediate liaison for the ship and her needs, is subordinate to the Boston SUPSHIPS (Supervisor of Shipbuilding, Conversion, and Repair) and the Navy Department's headquarters in Washington. The understanding is that the Boston office, being there on location, should make the direct recommendations and active decisions—with the advice and consent of the Navy Department and the Naval Sea Systems Command (NAVSEA). This is the logical loop in the chain—but, like all loops, they can rotate in both directions, and this explains my position in the system when I was designated by the Washington U.S. Navy's NAVSEA office to do the overall assessment of *Constitution*'s structures. This sort of injection might have upset some of the previous line of thought on the Boston end; if it did, I was not aware of it. The past few years have seen many, many more man-hours spent on the problems of *Constitution*'s aging by the Boston office and their staff than by NAVSEA and its Ship's Structures Division. Nevertheless, I suppose it is good engineering practice to step back from the drawing board and ask advice or help from someone from out of town.

So, in making judgments and offering recommendations for repairs, I had more to do than just weigh and evaluate the prior advice that had been filtering into the Navy Department. I spent some time in Boston inspecting and examining the ship itself as well as specimens of wood and fastenings withdrawn from the ship. I was also able to meet the people in the Boston office, including the Supervisor of Shipbuilding, Captain Sam Gagliano, USN, and participate in a most satisfying informal conference with two men who are as close as anyone to the ship's problems: Donald Turner, the resident superintendent of *Constitution*'s maintenance and repair, and Peter W. Witherell, Naval Architect in the office of SUPSHIPS Boston. While the three of us come from divergent backgrounds, and our opinions and ideas were not always in agreement, we were together in our understanding of the ship's problems if not the solutions. Because of our different experiences and expertise—Turner's with the day-to-day knowledge of the ship's condition, Witherell's theoretical and research-test input, and my own in historic ship structures—our discussions resulted in a constructive mix of information and ideas that could be applied to the old ship's repairs and, hopefully, her restoration.

In addition to the documents by P. W. Witherell already mentioned, the Navy Department had supplied another study by Mr. Witherell—the report of the model-test results of a so-called "composite space frame," a proposed additive preventive structure, and its effects on a structural model of *Constitution*—both models built to the same 1:16 scale. This report was significant mainly because of the considerable expense of providing the models and the study and research time involved. On the other hand, I did not find the results and recommendations significant or advisable, with my apologies to Mr. Witherell.

My lack of enthusiasm for the model test stems from several directions. Its main purpose was to provide the elaborate model mechanisms study as a basis for prescribing a frame structure within the ship to prevent deformation. My first objection is with the scaled structure model of the ship. The model, composed of transverse frames and external wales, is doubtless correct in its configuration—but it does not duplicate the ship's structural members. The model's frames are overdimensioned and spread out, omitting perhaps 60 percent of the frames, and the external wales are not comparable to the ship's in number or location. There is no inner ceiling or external planking or decking. The latter three items provide over 70 percent of the longitudinal strength of the ship—the strength factor with which the test is concerned.

Secondly, the so-called composite space frame to be inserted is specified to be made of a very high-tech reinforced plastic material used in modern racing yachts—tri-axial fiberglass and graphite fiber. Neither its bonding characteristics nor related mechanical characteristics such as elasticity, thermal, and moisture moduli, are similar to those of the remaining ship's structure of wood. In short, the space frame's entire structure, as stiff and strong as may be designed, appears to be configured the same and doing the same job as a system of *diagonal frame riders* discussed earlier. Unlike the wooden frame riders, however, it introduces a new material and, therefore, undermines the uniform material continuity of the whole wooden structure. Finally, it fails to meet the criterion of historic authenticity, and this is a very important consideration in *Constitution*'s restorative program.

As noted, the recent survey work has included the examination and testing of such important structural components as plank fastenings and wood. The testing of random wood samples by the U.S. Forest Products Laboratory were of little value to the study of *Constitution*. They were of incorrect species of wood for the type of strength tests, and the tests were carried out by researchers who had no knowledge of ship structure. Finally, the reports from the Forest Products Laboratory contained no conclusions. The fastenings examination, conducted by a marine surveying consultant, Rick Farris, Inc., was more useful. It consisted of an "ultrasonic inspection" of the accessible hull and plank fastenings. This digital "flow detector" tested the accessible ends of the metal fastenings, which were with few exceptions found to be in good condition. These fastenings were tested on the inside only; the external ends will be tested when the ship is drydocked. The questionable fastenings were of iron, not copper, and were found mostly in the lower bolts and drifts, and those fastenings used in the hanging and dagger knees as well as breasthooks.

For their 1984 metallurgical tests of plank fastenings, the Portsmouth Naval Shipyard withdrew a random number of copper nails, $7/8$ inch in diameter and 15 inches long. The report showed some corrosion-etched rings about the circumference; these deterioration lines on the nails, indicating exposure to atmosphere and moisture, occurred at the juncture of plank and frame (Figure 4-2). The gripping surfaces were in good shape, however, and the corrosion rings were not deep—only 9 percent of the nail diameter.

Structural survey, and specific areas of concern

Let's now take a look at the ship's structure, beginning with the drawing of *Constitution*'s structural parts (Figure 4-2). The left side of this illustration is a transverse section at the middle body; the ship's body being symmetrical in theory, only one side is shown. On the right is a portion of the middle body's longitudinal section, from the inside out. The transverse section shows the three principal decks, the gun deck being the heaviest structurally.

Normally, the gun deck would be the "strength" deck, taking approximately the same stresses as the ship's bottom when moving in a seaway; however, this is not strictly true in this old structure, since the design made no allowance for movement (expansion or contraction) in the spar deck above. Consequently, the spar deck, being uppermost, would tend to take some of the stress due to longitudinal bending forces. The berth deck below would tend to take the least of these compressive and tensile stresses; this is because it is very near the ship's *neutral axis*. The neutral axis is that imaginary transverse axis where there is no tension or compression when the ship is submitted to bending forces of variable buoyancy, generally of waves at sea. In any case, these stresses exist whether the ship is moving in a sea among waves or whether she is tied to a wharf in still water. The first condition creates alternating dynamic stresses; the second, mostly static stress.

The most significant of the hull stresses are the longitudinal ones. In a wooden ship, these forces, particularly the alternating stresses, produce a factor unlike any in a land-based structure: a constantly working, fatiguing motion with a tendency to loosen fastenings, open up joints in scarfs and seams in adjacent planking, loosen caulking between planks or in rabbet joints, etc. Obviously this produces leaks, both in the bottom and in decks, and results in corrosion of fastenings, most notably in the ferrous metals. It also causes dampness where fungus proliferates and rot begins.

There is little that can be done about all of this—particularly in a poorly built ship. *Constitution* was certainly built well originally, but she is an old ship—and in her long life she has been extensively repaired, allowed to languish during layups at the hands of indifferent caretakers, rebuilt, restored, reconditioned, refurbished—and, as we noted in the previous chapter, she even became for one long voyage a livestock barn and stable.

However, to say there is little that can be done about *Constitution*'s present condition—as has been suggested by uniformed people satisfied with the status quo—is not altogether true. This will be the subject of Chapter Five.

In the longitudinal section shown in Figure 4-4, notice the structure of the backbone—the vertical assembly of lower timbers, beginning with the keel and keel shoe and keel rider, topped by the keelson and keelson rider. Nearly 8 feet in height, the backbone is crossed by the transverse floor timbers between keel rider and keelson. This is the equivalent of a structural beam, running longitudinally throughout the ship, with a web 8 feet high and flanges 1 foot wide. Some beam! Because it is made of white oak, the strongest species of North American wood, it would be sufficient enough support for a two-lane highway bridge span, if properly structured.

This drawing shows the other species of wood used in the construction of "Old Ironsides"—mostly white oak, with Douglas-fir decking and ceiling and live oak transverse frames. Live oak trees are relatively shorter than other oaks, with wider spread, and thus produce a greater selection of timbers with curvature suitable for constructing curved frames.

In the two sectional views of Figure 4-2 and in the longitudinal profile of Figure 4-4, one can see all of the structural assembly of wooden members that hold the ship in shape. These members, held together primarily by metal fastenings, have maintained the ship's structural integrity for two centuries in an exemplary fashion. We are not now looking at any

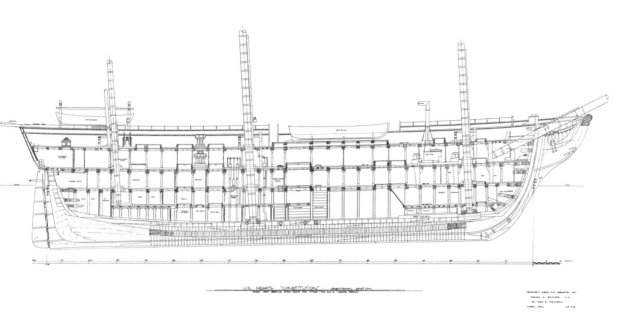

Figure 4-4. The entire longitudinal structural assembly of *Constitution* as she existed after the 1927-30 overhaul. There have been no known major changes to this inboard profile of the ship's structure since that time. The uppermost deck is the spar deck; the next one down is the gun deck, with the berth deck below.

failure of the system; rather, we are seeking a means to hitch her back a little more to her old and trimmer lines and provide some reasonably authentic way to hold her in shape.

During my own inspection of her hull in April of 1991 in the Charlestown Navy Yard, I was not struck by the need for urgent action. Her exterior and interior exhibit spaces, on the surface, were clean and shipshape—and still are. One had to look closely at things not immediately apparent, pointed to by the maintenance superintendent—areas that suggest distortion, decay, or suspicion.

For example, beginning on the spar deck, which was visibly scrubbed and polished, I examined a specific area on the port quarter where the transom joins the after gunwale, where a caulked seam approximately ½ inch to ⅝ inch in width was suspected to be slowly separating. The condition was identical port and starboard. The theory in Boston was that the transom was slowly canting aft, but I do not think this is the case. It is more likely related

Figure 4-5. The gun deck, looking aft; some distortion of the surface decking is visible in the foreground.

to tensile stress in the upper deck area. Whether this is simply a point of disagreement or a faulty analysis will be further discussed in Chapter Five.

I made my way down to the gun deck, which also looked to be in excellent condition—there was good ventilation, and everything seemed to be freshly painted. However, a photo taken at this time—Figure 4-5—shows a significant symptom of deck distortion on the starboard side, looking aft, at approximately Stations 13 and 14 on gun deck level. Quite possibly, this deck distortion is part of the general hull deformation due to hogging stress transmitted through the vertical structure.

The underdeck structure, Figure 4-6, shows a common type of shrinkage separation between a diagonal or dagger knee and a deck beam. There is also visible evidence of cracks in one of the upper heavy longitudinal ceiling planks, called clamps, under the deck beam, with the fracture extending both forward and aft of the dagger knee. This plank failure may be a symptom of possible tensile failure caused when tension in the hull in this area tries to stretch the wood.

My inspection progressed to the berth deck, where there is another deck distortion, shown in Figure 4-7, on the port side halfway from center, 20 to 30 feet aft of the foremast. It appears to be a result of the same general

Figure 4-6. Looking at the underdeck, we see a dagger knee against a deck beam, showing separation where it has withdrawn approximately ¼ inch. The longitudinal ceiling plank (beam clamp) shows several fractures indicating tensile failures in upper longitudinals where they are farther from the neutral axis.

hull deformation mentioned above. On this same deck, the nicely fashioned mast boot on the foremast shows some separation (Figure 4-8), apparently resulting from deck movement rather than mast movement. Going forward at this level into the space adjacent to the inner stem piece or *stemson*, I found that the breasthook showed very little indication of movement or separation. One of eight, this breasthook is the fifth down from the spar deck. It is a massive, natural-grown crook, or knee, canted down slightly from horizontal. Just aft of the stemson, some of the Douglas-fir inner ceiling had been scraped clear of paint. In Figure 4-9 the ceiling appears to be in reasonably good shape, with the riveted heads of the copper fastenings showing. There is evidence of some, but not serious, grain checking. The darker portion of a seam appears to be a localized area of decay, which is a symptom of local wood rot and must be noted for replacement, as well as for the source of dampness.

Figure 4-7. This photo of the berth deck, looking forward, shows bulging similar to that of the gun deck, shown in Figure 4-5.

In the hold area, below the orlop, approximately halfway between the fore- and mainmasts, a single strake of ceiling plank has been removed to expose the ship's transverse frames (Figure 4-10). These are original live oak frames, and they show the holes of the many fastenings that have penetrated them over the years of repair and restoration work. Looking to future restorations, there is serious concern as to the location of new plank fastenings and/or fastenings for additional interior structure. Without

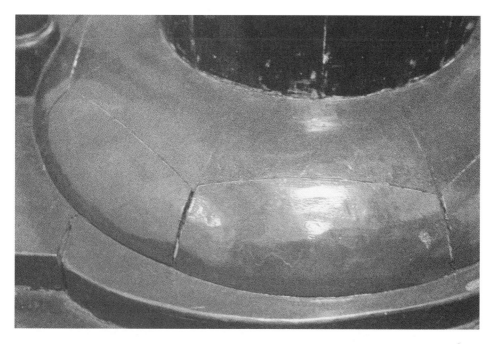

Figure 4-8. This nicely fashioned mast wedge/boot at the gun deck level shows a separation that indicates movement of the deck about the masts.

further study of transverse frames as yet uncovered, it is impossible to draw a definitive conclusion about their conditions. This situation must be carefully studied.

After checking other portions of the ship below decks, I found compressive bends in several of the vertical centerline stanchions from the keelson to deck beams; these are symptomatic of hogging stress.

As seen from the surface, from the spar deck to the ballast hold, the ship's material condition appears to be very good, when viewed through the framework of her age. Everything is clean and shipshape, light, and well-ventilated; there is no odor or mustiness or any suggestion of deterioration. The signs of age, evident in the visible deformation in deck bulges and bowed stanchions, do not strike me as critical.

However, when I am aboard a wooden vessel with painted surfaces, I

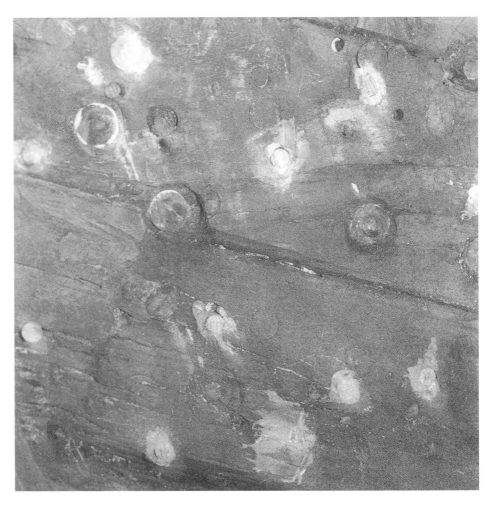

Figure 4-9. The inner ceiling planking in the end of the ship toward the stemson (inner stem) shows the wood to be in relatively good condition where it has been scraped clear of paint, with the riveted heads of the copper fastenings showing. The darker area at a seam shows some localized decay.

can't help but be concerned about what problems the paint may be covering. From her spar deck on down, *Constitution*'s surfaces seem to be painted throughout. This type of shipkeeping is commendable in many ways: it makes for cleanliness and easy maintenance, and it's psychologically more pleasant to live with. The negative side is that paint not only builds

Figure 4-10. In the ballast hold area below the orlop deck, approximately halfway between the fore and main masts, a strake of ceiling has been removed, exposing part of the transverse frames in this area. These original live-oak frames are riddled with holes from previous fastening, and there is some concern as to future replacement of planking. It is a situation that will require an improved system of fastening when the next replanking occurs.

up in both weight and dimension, it also can mask wood deterioration and the condition of connected parts and fastenings. In my opinion, much of the paint on this historic ship should be removed.

Shipshape—but how strong?

From the inside, then, *Constitution*'s present aesthetic appearance is very good and convincingly shipshape. Comparing this to her appearance in 1812, however, we confront a different sort of problem—her lack of homogeneity.

You must understand that *Constitution* is not only the oldest large wooden ship afloat, she is presently an incongruous assembly of wood of different origin, age, and species. While spending much of the last half of her life weathering alongside, she has been repaired, restored, disassembled, and re-formed—in random order. In this extensive collection of ship timber, there is no homogeneity of material such as there is in a metal ship. Simply put, the lack of material continuity prevents the desirable transmittal of stress, and thus undermines the uniformity of predictable results. Further, wooden ship timbers are worked by hand tools, for the most part, to dimensions called *scantlings*, where tolerance is reliably in the order of ¼ inch or so in large timbers, compared to tolerances of millimeters or hundredths of an inch for metal. This variation in wood is often aggravated by unforeseen flaws: for example, changes caused by knots, uneven wood grain, and weathering as the ship grows with her repairs over the years.

A ship is often thought of as a hollow, box-like girder with a top, bottom, and sides. With a steel ship, if we measure the strength of this girder, we've got an accurate measurement of the ship's overall strength. With wooden ships, however, because of the lack of uniformity and consistency of material, we have no rational approach to the measurement or numerical analysis of the ship's girder strength. For various reasons, wooden ships historically were *overbuilt* in timber and plank dimensions. As a result of traditional shipbuilding methods, unchanging customs, and arbitrary rules, we find ships of the past to be too heavy and full of much unnecessary timber. From the hindsight of today's technology, we must view some of this overbuilding with tolerance; yesterday's shipwrights lacked our efficient tooling, mechanical systems, adhesive systems, and the abundant assortment of metal fastenings available today. By "metal," I mean the steel and/or saltwater-resistant alloys. Of course, iron and bronze nails used in shipbuilding have been around since the fourth century B.C., but they were nonuniform—forged by hand and driven without the benefit of predrilled holes. The original fastenings in *Constitution*—heavy copper nails and long drift bolts—were made under contract by the famous metalsmith Paul Revere. (His contract agreement for the thousands of fastenings was fairly substantial at $3,820. Today, on the antique-collector's market, just one of these nails, confirmed as original, might well bring a higher figure than that.) It is said that all of the original Revere copper "bolts" (fastenings) were removed in the 1873 restoration, but I find this doubtful. Even though nearly all of the external planking was removed above the waterline, as well as much below, the heavy drift bolts holding together centerline timbers, knees, etc., remained.

Although we are unable to make an assessment of *Constitution*'s hull girder strength, the ship has been maintained comparatively better than others, such as USS *Constellation*'s 1850s incarnation, which shows hogging in the magnitude of some 4 feet. There are many ships of the same vintage lying aground in the Falkland Islands whose girder structure is essentially intact, though much of their planking is gone. As these hulks slowly decay and die, their backbones hold together down to the last timber assembly without much loss of shape. This, of course, proves little, considering that the ship's girder is essentially the deck, sides, and bottom of an integral assembly.

In this respect, I have a strong suspicion that while *Constitution*'s lower (berth) and upper (spar) decks are essentially continuous as the gun deck, although differing in dimensions, there is presently—after her various restorations—no clear *strength* deck in her girder. Since her original design, her sides have been increased in height throughout, caused mostly by adding solid bulwarks and increasing their heights for better deck crew protection. This additional bulwark has added some 6 feet of vertical height to her hull girder side dimension (see Figure 4-4). There is little allowance for expansion. Although the bulwark has openings and some discontinuity, the expansion stress is present. This, I believe, produces the movement in the spar deck, which in turn produces separations both forward and aft at the transom and stem head.

Correcting the deformities—some recommendations

In view of her age and deformities as described, I believe *Constitution*'s overall health is essentially good. This may sound like saying that a person of 90 years or more who is bright and conversational and ambulatory is in good health. With this ship, it is more than that.

The approaches I recommend for *Constitution*'s structural improvement and maintenance in my assessment for the Navy's Ship Structure's division will be reviewed in the following chapter. I think these approaches must be viewed from the assumption that much of the hull distortion may be satisfactorily removed and the hull returned reasonably close to its original form.

Assuming that the remaining hogging and other hull bottom distortion can be removed, the hull girder should be strengthened inside by one of several means that is as consistent with authentic 18th-century ship structure as is feasible. The problems are essentially three: the upward distortion in the backbone, the widening in the original beam dimension, and the corresponding decrease in vertical dimension (evident in the compression or bowing shape of the interior stanchions, together with reported loss of deck crown). I further believe that there is some sagging in the bilges, with corresponding but increased hollow in the garboard strakes.

This distortion may be more easily understood when seen in a graphic form, as in Figure 4-11. This illustration superimposes two body plans of *Constitution*—William Doughty's body plan of 1794, overlaid with the most recent authentic delineation available from the Navy Department, lines drawing No. 24473, September 1931, which is in agreement with the table of offsets done at the same time. As in previous overlay drawings of the ship included in this book, the common line of coincidence is the rabbet line on the keel. In this case, both body plans are shown to the outside of the planking. The solid lines are those from the Navy Department's drawing; the dashed lines are those from the original Doughty design drawing.

The station section lines from the forward perpendicular show that by 1931 a distinct excessive breadth had developed in the waterline waist belt all the way aft through Station 19. However, as we move down from the waterline flotation area toward the garboard area near the keel, the situation reverses; the original designed surface of the hull moves outside

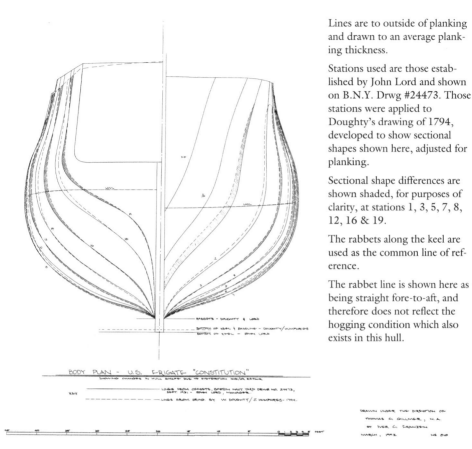

Lines are to outside of planking and drawn to an average planking thickness.

Stations used are those established by John Lord and shown on B.N.Y. Drwg #24473. Those stations were applied to Doughty's drawing of 1794, developed to show sectional shapes shown here, adjusted for planking.

Sectional shape differences are shown shaded, for purposes of clarity, at stations 1, 3, 5, 7, 8, 12, 16 & 19.

The rabbets along the keel are used as the common line of reference.

The rabbet line is shown here as being straight fore-to-aft, and therefore does not reflect the hogging condition which also exists in this hull.

Figure 4-11. An overlay of the original body plan sections on the most recent body plan, drawn from offsets taken off by Lieutenant John Lord in 1931. It is reasonable to believe that these changes in the shape of the ship over 134 years still exist, perhaps in larger dimension.

of the 1931 configuration. This change in shape is understandable as the result of a continuous *hogging*. Regarding the ship as a simple hollow tube, its reaction under a bending moment is roughly analogous to bending a beer can: its sides swell out as the top and bottom (opposite sides) become closer. The ship form is a little more complex, but the change in shape is similar—the breadth increases along the waist, and the garboard areas near the keel curve upward and inward. This bilge distortion may be helped along by the additional weight of the ship's guns along the sides of the gun deck. If we look at a side view, the distortion would be evident in the upward and inward curvature at the keel, which is recognized as the hogged keel—even though it occurs throughout the body of the ship as well. Unfortunately, there is no illustration adequate to scale the distortion very well.

In Figure 4-11, it is interesting to study the separation between the original Doughty body line and the 1931 body line at Station 1. This broader separation is in the forwardmost portion of the hull, and because no adjustment has been made for any hogging curvature of the keel, the station lines seem to show an exaggerated vertical difference between the two lines that may not exist. In fact, when the vertical separation is measured, it is exactly equal to the maximum hog of the keel amidships both in 1927 before docking and presently.

This difference in configuration between the two body plans (other than the adjustments described and the assumption, for plotting purposes, that the keel rabbet lines are straight for both plans) is most revealing. It is real evidence of the slow change in hull shape—the result of aging wood, of movement of wood against fastenings, as well as repairs, new structuring, restorations, relaxing of rigging, interior alterations, and all of the other changes, recorded and unrecorded, over a span of 134 years. As of this writing, we have added 61 more years. What is her waistline now? From this present vantage point, there is no reason to believe that it is greatly different. The keel hogging, which was said in 1931 to have been nearly removed (although the means of measuring it accurately were not available), has returned to the pre-restoration amount, or close to it.

I believe that the hull's shape, aside from hogged keel, can be restored and maintained by some form of frame riders and a limited number of diagonal riders. If such a procedure, as discussed in Chapter Five, is indeed undertaken and properly executed, it is as valid an assurance as any that the ship's more handsome, near-original shape can be held.

I have indicated that the hogged keel is part of the overall hull distortion. Keel deflection, within limits, is part of a wooden hull's natural deflection. It is also reversible. Most new wooden vessels naturally take on a hogging of the keel to some degree when they first become waterborne. It has been estimated that the frigates of the *Constitution*-class had keel deflections of 3 to 4 inches in their first year of operation. As a ship ages, this condition is bound to increase, and it has been well recorded in *Constitution*'s maintenance history.

The measurements indicate that *Constitution*'s keel deflection is 14.75 to 15 inches, with the prognosis that it may still be increasing. This may seem a disturbing enough amount, but the histories of other old ships suggest that the distortion will continue to increase to more alarming proportions with little or improper maintenance and repair. A most visible example is *Constellation* in Baltimore Harbor. Her hull is approximately 140 years old, compared with *Constitution*'s nearly 200 years, and the hogging distortion is estimated to be between 38 and 40 inches. I doubt this is all caused by keel distortion; *Constellation* has never been properly restored and her basic structure is in questionable condition.

I do not believe *Constitution*'s keel deflection has become critical, but as a reflection of overall hull distortion with the probability of increasing toward an intolerable condition, it must be arrested. There is no way to determine whether there is a limit beyond which the distortion would be critical or threatening.

My ship inspection adequately confirmed the hull's deformation, and the overlaid body plans (Figure 4-11) indicate the results of the forces at work. The distortion of the gun deck and berth deck, and the bowed stanchions and increased beam, all taken together with the keel hogging of about 15 inches, indicate that the hull has sagged along its middle-body bilges while rising longitudinally along the center, adjacent to the keel, producing a hogged keel. It is my best judgment that this problem must be dealt with as a significant priority. As for the crowning of the deck, this is a condition that naturally takes place over time, produced by local stresses such as the unequal loading of the gun battery outboard on both sides.

This additional problem is not evident in the ship except for the disuniformity in localized areas.

To continue with the overall assessment, I'll review the other problems I noticed in inspecting the ship, in order of their significance.

The apparent separation at the spar deck level at the after quarters and the stem, a symptom of the whole hull's flexure about the neutral axis, is logically most evident at the extreme locations—that is, at the uppermost level, in the foremost and aftermost extremities.

As for the evident separation of the hanging knees (Figure 4-12) and dagger knees (Figure 4-6) at the surfaces of deck beams, that is the nature of wooden knees. Whether or not they are naturally grown and of considerable strength for wood, sooner or later they will show some separation at the surface of contact. I do not recommend that these knees be refastened, but rather that they be removed and replaced by steel knees, fabricated to fit very closely—this to be done only after the ship's hull distortion and deck

Figure 4-12. The berth deck of *Constitution* as it appeared in 1900. This photograph clearly shows the large wooden hanging knees, which are very susceptible to decay—particularly due to leaky deck seams and the scuppers directly above. Such knees also shrink across the grain, separating from their original close fit against the beams and ceiling.

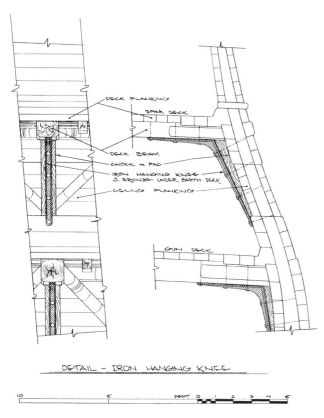

DECK PLANKING
SPAR DECK
DECK BEAM
CHOCK or PAD
IRON HANGING KNEE
S. BRONZE UNDER BERTH DECK
CEILING PLANKING
GUN DECK

DETAIL - IRON HANGING KNEE

Figure 4-13. This drawing describes the more advisable use of iron or bronze knees. Metal knees such as these have none of the vulnerability of the wooden knees shown in Figure 4-12; they are also historically correct, used in other ships of *Constitution*'s time.

restorations have been made. Metal knees (see Figure 4-13) are quite authentic for *Constitution*'s historic period. As an example of precedent in American historic ships, Captain John Paul Jones's ship *Bonhomme Richard* was built with wrought-iron hanging knees throughout. Most large French and British warships were also so built. The installation of metal knees is a further means of arresting hull distortion in the movement of wood.

Earlier in this chapter I observed that the distorted decks are indirectly part of the overall hull distortion. The decks themselves, particularly the spar deck and gun deck, are in need of replacement. Because the spar deck is farthest removed from the ship's neutral axis, it should be built so that it allows for some movement under compression and tension. I would further recommend that it not be painted, but kept well caulked and bright and regularly wetted down and scrubbed to keep it tight. Such a surface can be better monitored for the beginning of any deterioration or localized decay. Douglas-fir planking would be my choice for the redecking, rather than using tropical woods, which would be very expensive and unauthentic.

There is no notable deterioration of the inner ceiling, and if the wood proves sound upon further inspection in drydock, it should be left in place, repairing only locally. The exterior planking is largely covered, either by copper sheathing (bottom) or layers of paint (topsides). The paint should be completely removed for thorough inspection. Before drydocking, the upper planking farthest from the neutral axis and along the ship's middle body should be removed, particularly along the bulwarks in the ship's waist. I believe some of this planking is redundant. It was installed when the ship was very new (1800–01) and later as a cosmetic addition meant to make the hogging less noticeable. It is also recommended that the strakes above gunports amidships on the gun deck be removed before drydocking.

The ballast consists predominantly of stone mixed with some recently added lead; the exact ratio is unknown. When the vessel is in drydock, I would advise against removing the ballast immediately, since the ballast weight would help reduce the ship's hogging. However, after drydocking her, I think a more precisely measured and fixed ballast, such as lead pigs, should be installed.

Finally, so that detailed inner bottom inspections can be made, the hold areas should be cleared of temporary bulkheads and living-area structures. It is here in the hold that much of the necessary restoration and preventive restructuring will most likely take place.

"Can she be restored?"

In discussing the problems affecting "Old Ironsides," I have based the above determinations on visible evidence as well as analysis and comparisons of things past. As one may clearly see, the ship is distorted in hull shape both above and below water. She has been reconstructed and repaired many times over many years, sometimes carefully, sometimes ill-advisedly. She is not the good and homogeneous ship that she once was. She has lost much of her original beauty, strength, and character. The question now is, "Can she be restored?" Structurally, the answer is clearly yes. But there is the more difficult problem of gaining enough public support to fund such a project.

There was a time, in 1830, that a mere poem ignited the public spirit that prompted a restoration. Again, in 1927, it was a public response led by schoolchildren that set the money machines to flow. Can we expect one more show of public emotional force to shake the sedentary Congress? Perhaps, but at the moment the outlook is bleak. Unhappily, there is no unidirectional or single-minded authority to oversee or merely to support a restorational movement. There are some who would rig and sail her again, others who violently oppose such an idea. Some would haul her ashore as a monument preserved under glass. And finally, alas, there are those who would let her rot—those (too many, I fear) who have never even heard of *Constitution*, and to whom this book is commended.

In the final chapter, I hope I can direct positive thinking toward some means to repair and strengthen "Old Ironsides." We cannot turn time backward, but we can perhaps restrain time's progressive disintegration. We might restore some of *Constitution*'s original form and handsome countenance. Certainly it's worth trying. Once this grand ship successfully lifted the American public's spirit and strengthened its resolve toward surmounting the seemingly impossible task of shaking off British domination. She is the only and oldest symbol of our resolve not to submit to the tyranny of terrorists. Perhaps, with her restoration, we could restore some of this national pride.

5

The Restoration Question

To have a firm sense of where we are going, we must also know where we have been. This holds true in facing the problems inherent in any restoration of *Constitution*. To help get us oriented I have prepared a special profile delineation of the old ship, Figure 5-1—a comparative analysis of her appearance in 1795 and 1926.

Changes over time

The drawing is based on the most recent and correct inboard profile of the ship, done by Lieutenant John Lord, who was in charge of the 1927–30 reconstruction. These are the solid lines in the profile, and we must assume that they are still representative. Over them, in dashed lines, I have drawn the Humphreys/Doughty profile of 1795.

Beginning at the stem and bow head, we can see a remarkable difference in structure over the span of some 130 years. The handsome curvature of her original late-18th-century stemhead, which carried the graceful trailboards from her bow to the scrolled figurehead base, has been completely replaced by the enormous upward and outward extension of the present

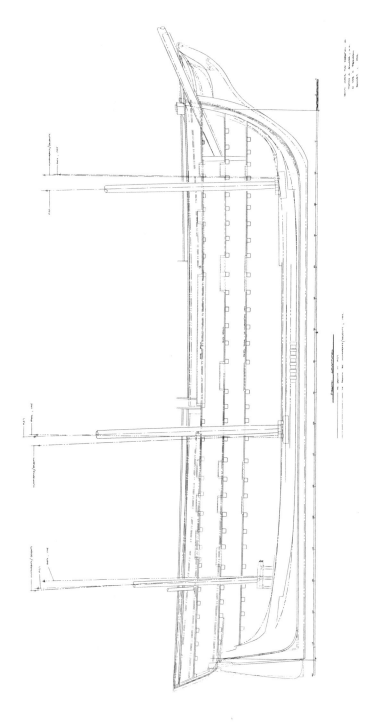

Figure 5-1. This composite drawing, with the 1794 profile (dashed lines) overlaid on a recent drawing (solid lines) at the same scale, compares the original frigate *Constitution* with the ship as she exists today. No attempt is made to show the hogging or distortion that is now in the keel. Note the difference in size and shape of the bow head as well as stem enlargement, and the difference in mast locations and their various angles of rake. The increased height of the bulwarks is significant in her lost sheerline.

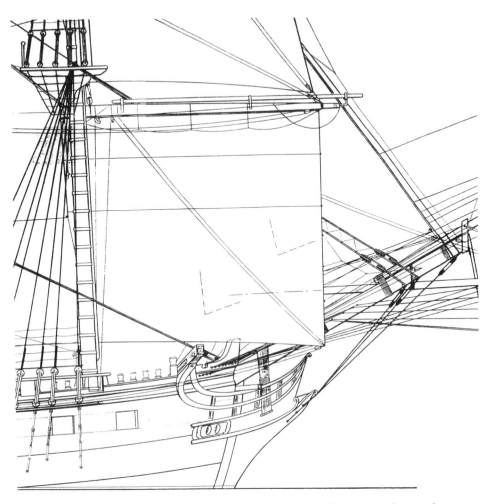

Figure 5-2. *Constitution*'s forward extremities, as originally designed, were her most impressive and handsome features. It is a pity that none of these features still exist. They are buried in time, plastered over by the successive repairs and reconstructions of nearly two centuries. They could be restored by skilled shipwrights—the plans still exist.

stemhead. The structure as it exists now is capped by an overwrought scrolled carving that looks nothing like the first one, which replaced the original figurehead after the Mediterranean collision in 1804—nor is it like any of the varying 19th-century scroll replacements (see Chapters Two and Three). All in all, the forward extremity is now a vastly exaggerated con-

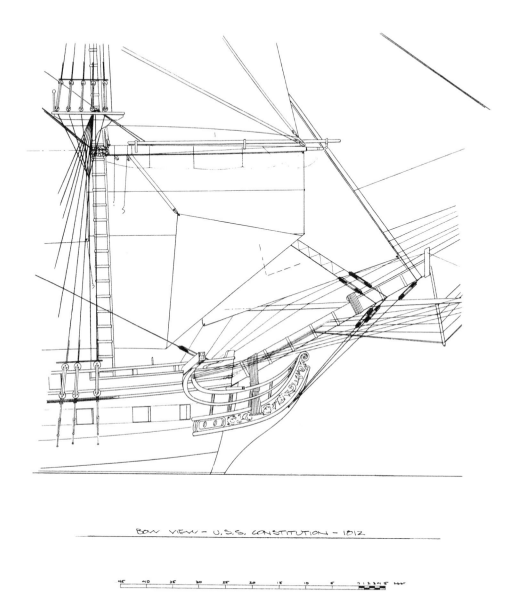

BOW VIEW - U.S.S. CONSTITUTION - 1812

Figure 5-3. To restore *Constitution*'s forward profile to its appearance in 1812 would be a good compromise, needing only a small amount of license in removing the old enclosure about the crew's head, which from its early inception after the turn of the 19th century grew more predominant over the years. The scrolled billethead would be perhaps more graceful than an attempt to reinvent the original figurehead; there is no record as to what it really looked like.

trivance that grew through years of reconstruction by indifferent artisans and misdirected carpenters. The head enclosure, which also has grown out of proportion, further emphasizes the overweight bow. This whole portion of the ship is grotesquely out of balance.

To bring back the simplicity and grace of her original concept, her stem-head and forward structure should be restored to something akin to her appearance in 1803–04 or 1812–15, as shown in Figures 5-2 and 5-3.

Returning to Figure 5-1 and our structural comparison, the bowsprit appears to be steeved up a bit higher than its original angle. But this position on the original Humphreys/Doughty base is unchanged.

The original stempost below the waterline was not as great in molded dimension as it is now, all the way to the keel. Much of the present stempost timber has been replaced and rescarfed so there is little of the original post remaining. The rabbet line, from the lower gripe of the stempost aft along the keel, is remarkably coincident with the first. This clearly reflects an important truth: that there is indeed an original keel, as executed by Joshua Humphreys and his builder, Edmund Hartt. The keel measurements in both the sided dimension and molded dimension (vertical) are the same as they were at first and the wood is still intact. A keel is not a thing that can be removed from a ship without dismantling the whole. This timber shows its age and its maintenance scars, but it is still solid. The after junction with the sternpost at the keel has been changed to a curved rabbet; otherwise, the rabbet in the sternpost also coincides.

The basic benchmarks for this comparison, in addition to the coinciding keel rabbet, are the forward and after perpendiculars. Other close or coincident parts and lines are the keelsons, top and bottom. The spar deck and the gun deck agree closely as far aft from the bow as the mainmast; aft of that, the sheer has been flattened out. Moving up to the sheer rail at the forecastle and quarterdeck, considerable height has been added to the bulwarks—approximately 2¼ feet at the main gangways opposite the mainmast, and constant on aft to the transom. These apparent changes in freeboard only add to the visible height, for the true freeboard—the height above the maximum waterline of the weather deck at its lowest point—is substantially the same.

One of the most striking diversions from the original design is in the locations of the masts. The foremast step has been moved aft about 2 feet 4 inches. At the deck it is 3 feet 2 inches farther aft, showing an increased rake aft of more than 2½ degrees; this results in a total aftward change of approximately 5½ feet to the mast's fore top. The mainmast, to the contrary, has been moved forward and closer to the foremast, with the mast-step center moved about 2 feet 3 inches forward on the keelson. The rake has remained about the same. The mizzenmast shows the least change, having been moved aft only about 13 inches and raked only slightly less than the original design indicated. It is remarkable that it is so close, considering the various rigging adjustments, mast replacements, and "seaman's eye" judgments in the 131 years separating these two plans. Also shown in this comparison are the locations of the masts as drawn by Josiah Fox. Although Fox, it has been decided, was not the ship's designer, his hull drawings are available and very similar in profile. His mast placements are close to the original in the foremast but not comparable to either in the main or mizzen.

The sheer rail line of the original Humphreys design shows a graceful curve, rising at the stern to nearly the same position as the present rail. As I have mentioned earlier, the bulwarks were built up over the years—first for more protection in combat, and subsequently as the result of reconstructions in the spar and gun decks. It is clear in the comparative profiles of Figure 5-1 that both of these decks have been dropped from the middle body aft, eliminating the true deck sheer. This alteration was probably ordered by one of the captains in the 1830s' overhaul, for the purpose of creating a flatter platform for the guns. There is no structural requirement that the deck line follow the sheerline of the ship. The rising sheerlines of these decks were originally parallel, and in the newer profile they are still parallel. In any case, dropping the decks aft created a small problem

Figure 5-4. Today's plain, undecorated quarter galleries reflect, if nothing else, the lack of present-day awareness of *Constitution*'s original decorative detail. It should be restored to show the original carvings of oak leaf garlands that surrounded the windows, as well as a stern transom restoration.

for *Constitution*'s rudderport, which had to be lowered. We can see that the lower transom is not coincident with the original.

All of these changes to the lower stern assembly detracted from the clean and attractive stern of the original design; they also required that the tiller's shape be altered, with the addition of a "dogleg" to clear the deck beams of the gun deck aft. The new rudderhead was moved forward as well. The present rudder does not match the original, of course; its center of effort is lower and farther aft, which would produce a somewhat "harder" helm under sail. Viewing the whole profile comparison, we must admit that the ship has aged with some loss of grace.

Constitution's present transom is slightly farther aft than in the original design—again, likely the result of reconstructing the after portions of the decks. The gun deck level had originally held the gallery windows of the commodious cabin.

The upper transom and quarter galleries, once heavily decorated with expertly executed carving contemporary with the 1803–04 period, were modified over the years, mostly due to their vulnerability to battle damage, which occurred a number of times during the War of 1812. The first and most notable change to the transom came as a result of the famous, very tense chase by the British squadron in 1812 (see Chapter Two), when Captain Isaac Hull found he had no gun ports aft to defend this threatened approach—so he ordered gun crews to carve some out with axes and muscle stern chasers into position. The ship's present upper transom (see Figure 5-4), now restored without carvings to the 1812 period, has three stern gun ports on her spar deck level for stern chase protection.

A restoration benchmark of 1803–04

To return the ship to her original or early-19th-century appearance, I would suggest several priorities, both structural and cosmetic.

The basic recommended changes are structural: for her restoration of strength and the prevention of recurring hull distortion and hogging. The most urgent of these, I believe, is to restore the hull configuration in the ship's buoyant body. This is a drydock job, and will be discussed in further detail later in this chapter. Next in order of importance is restoration of the upper body. The planking along the ship's waist above the gun ports should be removed. The gun deck and the spar deck abaft the mainmast should be replaced, together with the deck beams along the original deck lines. The planking along the upper middle body and aft from the waterline up should be restored, with bulwarks limited to the original profile design.

As far as cosmetic changes are concerned, the first and foremost should be to restore the grace of her forward structure—the stemhead, bow head, and trailboards—according to the Humphreys/Doughty design. In the absence of any definitive drawings of the first figurehead, an appropriate scrollhead should be put in its place.

The stern, including the quarter galleries and the transom decoration, should be restored according to the original design. The sail plan and outboard hull profile shown in Figure 2-12 are a close approximation of the 1803–04 period recommended as a benchmark for her restoration.

"Wooden armor" and transverse strength

I have said very little about the strength of the ship's *transverse* structure, and its apparent weakening. Although the deformation of her bottom is a visible symptom of loss of strength, a ship's transverse strength is typically subordinate to the strength of the more significant *longitudinal* truss. The two are interdependent. If we reduce hogging to a minimum, the sagging bilges should be corrected—unless there is something in the way. As for the live oak frames, these are the primary foundation members that created the ship's geometric configuration, and so any restoration must avoid the temptation of renewing or replacing a great number of them. Because the frames are very closely spaced (see Figures 3-3 and 4-2), forming a nearly solid wall of framing beneath the planking, frame replacement is very difficult and sensitive, and should only be necessary where the frame is extremely decayed.

Let us take a closer look at the remarkable, wall-like impact strength that existed in "Old Ironsides"—at least in her youth. Her legendary deflection of cannonballs was not all that unusual—there is no doubt that a 74 could also resist cannon fire. But her strength confounded the British; mainly, they said that *Constitution* was built like a 74-gun ship-of-the-line, with an inference that it was not fair to do that. Of course, she did not carry as many guns as a 74. On the other hand, the *Constitution*-class frigate was designed to sail faster than a 74. The British complaint about American-built frigates approximating 74-gun ships-of-the-line is not far off base. It was Humphreys's strategic design to build the *Constitution*-class as he did—to be large enough to defeat any European frigate and to sail well enough to escape from a multiple force, or a ship of obvious superiority.

We can still enjoy the complaints of the nonvictorious after so many years. As Peter Tadfield writes in *Guns at Sea* (Hugh Evelyn Ltd., London: 1973):

Although both these vessels [*Constitution* and *Guerrière*] were classed as frigates there was little similarity between them; the *Constitution* class had been built expressly to "possess in an imminent degree the advantage of sailing, that separately they would be superior to any European frigate—that they would never be obliged to go into action but on their own terms. . . ." This specification was fulfilled. The *Constitution* was longer than the *Guerrière* by 17 feet; she carried 15 long 24-pounders each side on the main deck to the *Guerrière*'s 14 long 18-pounders. . . .

The extraordinary shock which the news of this action produced in Britain can only be explained by their faith that a British ship was bound to triumph as by Divine right: [In 1812, the *London Times*] remarked that "the spell of victory has been broken." And finally, after *Constitution*'s and her sister ships' continued successes, the *London Times* further editorialized, "The public will learn, with sentiments which we shall not presume to anticipate, that a third British frigate has struck to an American. . . . Can these statements be true?" The *Naval Chronicle* stated that "an English frigate rated 38 guns should undoubtedly, barring extraordinary accidents, cope successfully with a 44-gun ship of any other nation."

Let's examine this "wooden armor" capability a bit further. How fast does a "hot" baseball pitcher throw a ball? Close to 95 miles an hour, and it almost makes a sizzling sound as it clears the plate. With a fastball like that, especially thrown just a little inside, a good pitcher can intimidate the best of batters. Compared with a 24-pound cannonball fired with a standard powder charge, however, our fastball is not in the same league. When it leaves the gun's muzzle, that iron orb is traveling close to 580 miles per hour. When it strikes the ordinary oaken side of a frigate's hull— such as that of *Guerrière*, which *Constitution* destroyed in less than 40 minutes—it shatters its way through, slowing down only a little. Often such momentum carried the cannonball in one side and out the other, leaving a path of destruction all the way.

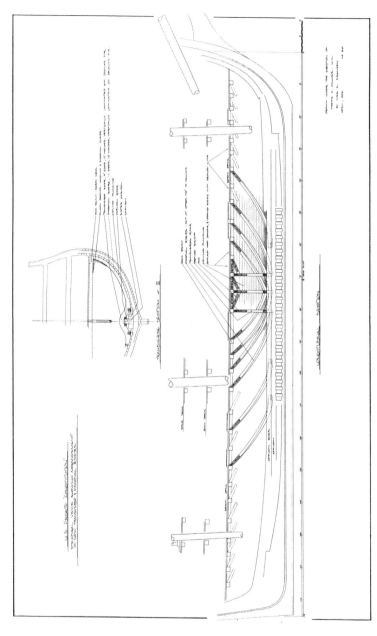

Figure 5-5. Much consideration has been given to the restoration of hull shape and its improved resistance to hogging. It is my recommendation that a modified form of the traditional transverse and diagonal riders, shown here, be used. Similar riders were originally specified by Joshua Humphreys in his descriptions of the 44-gun frigates; they were referred to again in 1927 by Lieutenant John Lord in his transverse structural drawing (Figure 1-7). In spite of this, there is no evidence that they were ever installed. Such an inner structure of built-up timbers could be the anti-deformation panacea that *Constitution* has needed for so long.

Yet it is true that "Old Ironsides" stopped cannonballs. They variously were deflected, bounced off, or stuck in her exterior planking. And why not? The hull's thickness, above the waterline in the waist and middle length, was nearly 2 feet through a three-layer lamination of solid oak, live oak, and fir. This was backed on the inside by hanging knees, dagger knees, lodging knees, and deck beams (see Figure 1-7). As discussed in Chapter Four, there is some evidence that there was also an inner reinforcing bridge composed of diagonal frame riders (Figure 5-5), although these would have been below the waterline. Whether or not *Constitution* or any of her sisterships ever were constructed with these frame riders is still questionable. They were allegedly specified by Joshua Humphreys, but there is no evidence today that they were ever there or were ever later incorporated, as promised on Lieutenant John Lord's plan No. 35208 of February 1926.

These diagonal frame riders—as described by Lord on the plan (Figure 1-7), "six pairs per side, three forward of [centerline] of ship and three aft, s & p [starboard and port]" should be incorporated in the next restoration or reconstruction, after the ship has been drydocked and the hull deformation removed to a suitable extent. Together with midship transverse riders, the diagonal frame riders would assist the ship's transverse frames in maintaining the hull's body shape and to prevent the bilges from sagging and the backbone (keel and keelsons) from rising (hogging). They would further stiffen the hull transversely. If installed originally, they would have further enhanced the hull's legendary ability to absorb the impact stresses of cannonballs traveling at some 500 miles per hour.

Figure 5-5 illustrates a proposed arrangement of the frame rider systems. They need not be of sistered (lapped) timbers, as typical of 18th- and 19th-century wooden ship construction; yet they should be compatible and laid in snugly by laminating layers of fir. The transverse (cross-keel) frame riders must bridge across the top of the keelson to prevent the upward distortion of the garboard area when hogging stresses are imposed. The diagonal riders should run diagonally forward and aft, respectively, up from the keelson and from the midship area. I recommend that they slope upward at about a 45-degree angle to connect with dagger knees under the deck beam of the berth deck. They should be sided about 9 inches and molded 12 inches and lie on top of the newly restored and/or repaired ceiling, and be bolted through to new strakes of outer planking.

In this very fundamental and complex restructuring of the transverse strength, we must not forget the frames between the ceiling and exterior planking, for they too would be helped. We cannot expect these lapped assemblies of futtock pieces to perpetually resist oblique stresses and hold their original shape. This would be a reasonable expectation, perhaps, on a smaller vessel, where the buoyant forces are balanced by cargo loading and more homogeneous loading. But on a warship, with its heavy localized armaments, service compartments, outboard ordnance, and centerline emptiness, these odd distributions of extreme vertical forces require additional hull support.

And so I propose that the diagonal and transverse frame riders be comparably replaced or restored as described. The frames alone are and were intended to hold apart the inner and outer skins of the hull primarily for their "hollow girder" contribution to the longitudinal strength. They can still function well in that purpose.

Stability

So far, nothing has been said about the penultimate property of every ship: its stability as it floats in the sea. Not only is stability important in itself, but the ship's command must communicate its significance to the officers and crew. Today's professional, qualified-for-sea-duty naval officers come to a full understanding of ship stability from the academic study of naval architecture. However, two centuries ago stability was only roughly understood—mostly in an empirical way—by master shipwrights. The subject was just beginning to appear in books on naval architecture, and there were very few of these. One of the very first was published in France in 1776.[1]

The events leading up to a truly scientific study of ship stability were unrelated and rather accidental. There was in France in the 18th century an exceptionally gifted physical scientist named Pierre Bouguer. In the mid-1700s, Bouguer found himself aboard a ship on an expedition sponsored by the French government's Academie des Sciences de France that was to determine the length of one degree of the meridian at the equator (this was also the basis for establishing the metric system of linear measure, although the nearly simultaneous birth of the metric system and the metacentric principles had no tangible relation). Unaccustomed to and probably inspired by the ship's motion in a seaway, Bouguer became interested in ship stability. It was a seven-year expedition, and he had much time to reflect on the subject. The discomfort stimulated his scientific mind to probe the causes of ship motion, and the result was his theory of the meta-center, as described in Chapter One.

Upon his return home he prepared a dissertation, to become a landmark publication, called "A Treatise on Theoretical Shipbuilding." Published in 1746, the book ultimately became a cornerstone in the academic and scholarly approach to ship design. From this developed the theory and finite method of measuring *initial stability*, and describing righting moments and overall stability. Although we need not go deeply into these theories here, it is helpful to say that in 1795 Joshua Humphreys and William Doughty were undoubtedly aware of the meaning of *metacentric height* (the vertical distance between the center of gravity of the ship and its metacenter; it is a measure of the initial stability). By the last decade of the 18th century, experienced and talented shipwrights had received this new stability theory from European sources. Reports in the 16th- and 17th-century records of warships were replete with accounts of ships suddenly heeling over and sinking, even in protected harbors. Large ships, particularly warships, figure most often in these reports, the smaller ones being probably less noteworthy; the records reflect the merchant vessels' similar vulnerability merely by statements of "overdue," "missing at sea," etc.

The stability factors in a ship are generally invisible except perhaps to an experienced eye. But even the most expert eye is blind to the most important single element: the invisible locus of all *gravitational forces* within the ship. Called *center of gravity*, it is a point where all of the weight of the ship—its structure, its parts, everything on board, and everything built into it—is centralized into a single acting location. This total force of weight acts vertically downward from this point. On a floating ship, the total upward force is the *buoyancy*, and it opposes the gravitational force in an equal amount. The buoyant center on a floating ship at rest is directly under the center of gravity. They are in line until the ship is moved, responding to water motion, the wind in her sails, or moving/changing weights. The

Figure 5-6. This exceptionally rare and extremely valuable painting by the French artist Antoine Roux, dated 1802, shows a *Constitution*-class frigate riding out a fierce gale in the Mediterranean outside Marseille. It is controversial whether the ship is *Constitution* or her sistership, *President*. At any rate, she is snugged down with housed topmasts, jibboom, and lowered course yards—all evidence of good seamanship and knowledge of center-of-gravity control.

resulting separation between the lines of action through the center of buoyancy and the center of gravity is the core of the study of ship stability.

The captain's awareness of the location of the center of gravity is a measure of the ship's safety or security from the ominous results of instability. The captain and his well-trained crew can, within reasonable limits, control the location of the center of gravity and avoid allowing it to become too high. But nothing can be done in a practical way at sea about controlling the capricious center of buoyancy.

There is abundant evidence in the paintings and prints done several centuries ago—including those that survive from *Constitution*'s early days—that the sailors and commanders of seagoing vessels understood the importance of their ships' center of gravity. The use of ballast, for example, is perhaps the most significant example of the awareness of gravity, location of weight, and its effect on stability. This awareness is also evident in paintings of ships in storms and heavy weather. One very pertinent example is a beautiful painting by the French artist Antoine Roux of a United States frigate, either *Constitution* or *President* (Figure 5-6). The U.S. Naval Institute Photo Library file says it is "probably" *Constitution*; the U.S. Navy Photographic Center says it is *President*. Either way, the matter of identity is of small import. They are sisterships, and the painting is significant not only as an image of the *Constitution*-class of frigate in the early 1800s, but because it represents the ship rigged for maximum stability in heavy conditions.

This is an excellent painting—almost photographic, as are all of Roux's renderings. It is the date given in the title—1802—that for me identifies the ship as *President*. She is flying the Commodore's broad pennant as flagship. In 1803 *President* was relieved by Commodore Preble in *Constitution* as flagship of the Mediterranean squadron.

The ship is anchored in an obviously heavy storm. Her yardarms are all slung down, and the topmasts and the topgallant masts are housed (lowered to the extent of their doublings and shrouds); the jibboom is housed similarly. These are examples of lowering the tophamper weight to lower the center of gravity and hence maximize stability.

I have stated earlier that *Constitution* and her sisterships carried a very lofty rig, with topgallant poles riding high above the topmast. It is evident in this painting that all of the upper yardarms, the topgallant, and royal yards have been struck below. The heavy yards—the topsail yards and main, fore, and mizzen course yards—being too cumbersome to be quickly unrigged and lowered to deck, have been lowered as far as practical and braced up hard. The sails are tightly furled to minimize windage. It is fair to speculate that if the gale continued to worsen, the heavier yards would also be lowered all the way to the deck.

Whether the ship's commanding officer reasoned that he must lower the upper spars and bring down the yards to lower the weights and better his center of gravity we do not know. More likely, this course was a traditional act of good seamanship, as was recorded many years earlier, well before Pierre Bouguer defined the metacenter. For whatever reason, this excellent portrait shows the *Constitution*-class frigate maintaining her stability and preserving a more comfortable motion in a heavy sea.

Nothing has yet, in any recorded way, seemed ever to threaten *Constitution*'s stability.

We might examine this painting a bit further to check the details of a pre-1812 *Constitution* or one of her sisters. Much has been written about *Constitution*'s appearance before the War of 1812, a good deal of it contradictory. This painting by Antoine Roux has been little seen and less examined in publications. And while it most likely depicts the frigate *President*, only the less-significant details will vary.

Beginning forward, the figurehead shown by Roux appears to be an assembly of two figures, a taller and a shorter figure—perhaps a child beside an adult. Neither this figurehead nor the carver has been described in the historic literature. The figure may likely be a Greek mythological character, a popular image for ships in the early 1800s. It does not appear to be political, as were some figureheads, in attempting to follow the theme of the ship names.

Above the head rails, the enclosed head sides appear to be set back farther and were less obtrusive than they later became; the head structure has not yet grown to the ridiculous proportions that exist on *Constitution* today. The spar deck shows bulwarks along the ship's waist, pierced for cannon; these again are controversial in the historic literature and in the attempts to reconstruct *Constitution's* early appearance. In Figure 2-12 I have shown only the stanchions in wood with open rail waist on the spar deck. There are but two guns visible forward of the waist, but *Constitution* probably carried more guns to her Mediterranean station in 1803. The lightly built bulwarks were fitted between the gunwale stanchions quite likely in Malta before the siege of Tripoli. In the Roux painting there is clearly no construction forward of the gangway accommodating the iron stanchion work for holding the hammock nettings. This sort of iron stanchion would require a heavy bulwark base resembling that provided aft of the gangway opening. The painting shows only a light caprail over the gun ports, which further substantiates a lightly built bulwark. The purpose of this construction was mainly to discourage boarders from coming over the side amidships, where there was no rigging to slow them down and render them vulnerable in hand-to-hand combat.

There appear to be 15 cannons extending from the gun deck ports on the starboard side, seven aft of the gangway on the spar deck, and probably three on the starboard side forward. Assuming the guns are in place symmetrically according to custom, the frigate is carrying a battery of 50 guns. This was generally the habit of the *Constitution*-class frigates when on station at war.

Whether this painting is of *Constitution* or *President*, it is no doubt the most reliable guide to the appearance of our best frigates pre-1812. She is definitely shown in her working condition and not dressed up for ceremony. Aside from her figurehead and the closed-in waist rail, I believe the painting should be a major reference in the restoration efforts of "Old Ironsides."

Drydocking

Constitution has been drydocked more frequently in recent years than when she was in active service. There were no drydocks available in her early career; in fact, she was the first vessel of this class of ship to be dry-docked. In 1833 she was docked in the new drydock in Boston—the same dock she uses exclusively now. The schedule is irregular, but drydockings generally occur about every 10 years. By the time these lines are in print, her next drydocking will have taken place.

Drydocking is a bit more of a problem for "Old Ironsides" nowadays than it was in the past. Such an old ship is simply more vulnerable to damage. Her wooden hull, particularly the bottom/backbone, has deteriorated to an undetermined extent and is presumably more fragile. In any case, she must be drydocked very carefully.

In the 1926 photograph shown in Figure 5-7, the keel blocks and bilge blocks have been set up to receive her, and the empty dock is being flooded. In the distance is the ship herself, waiting for the gates to open. The fact that the keel blocks are being flooded over from the stern forward indicates that they are docking on a level waterline and the ship is heading in bow-first; and the dock is prepared for her to land keel-first, which is customary.

For a ship of *Constitution*'s age, I would reject the idea of a routine docking. Customary or not, an old wooden ship should not be drydocked with her initial weight on the keel only. Drydocking, in *Constitution*'s case, calls for the bilge blocks to be in place before the dock is fully pumped down so that the ship's weight is supported partially on her bilges. This is hopeful procedure, but it is doubtful that this or any drydock ever manages to get the bilge blocks fully wedged in place before the dock is dry. With her weight of a couple of thousand tons now possibly being a destructive force along the centerline of the ship, I would propose what I think is a better way.

Historically, ships built of wood or steel are supported when launched (or out of the water) along a substantial surface of their bilges, on both

Figure 5-7. This 1926 photo shows Drydock No. 1, Boston Naval Shipyard, being flooded to take *Constitution* (left background). The bilge blocks and body cradle timber forms are ready to move into the ship's underbody, and the keel blocks are in place and inclined to conform with her keel's aft-ward slope (drag). This was her docking for the 1927–30 restoration, described in Chapter Three.

sides of the keel only, by a structure similar to that shown in Figure 5-7—a structure with a longitudinal stringer on each side, pre-shaped to fit the curvature of the ship's bottom. Apparently, these bottom supports are to be forced inward to contact the ship's bottom when she is "safely" resting on the keel blocks. This is a very good idea, but for *Constitution*, considering the probable fragility of her backbone structure, I believe the sequence should be reversed. It would be more corrective to allow the hull to settle on bottom bilge supports first. I would recommend that the side stringer arrangement shown in the photograph be increased so as to have at least two shaped and blocked stringers on each side, for a more complete, cradle-like support. Such a structure would more gently accept and distribute the hull's weight, while supporting and restoring the distorted and sagging bilges. After the dock has been pumped down, the keel blocks could be wedged up to proper alignment, and in time could adjust and correct the hogged keel.

Bilge deformity could best be reversed as shown in the transverse section (Figure 5-8) by either the old (and crude) wedge system, or by a more controlled system of precut or laminated bilge forms that fit the appropriate sections. The forms would notch into the stringers at regular intervals along the cradle support. The supporting shores shown on the right ("Docking Plan B") would be preferable—using adjustable, steel tubular shores on screw jacks.

In essence, my best advice about docking this venerable ship during this last decade of the 20th century is to allow her to somehow come to rest easily on the rise of her bilges and avoid concentrating her great weight on her keel.

The need for restoration

It is perhaps too late—without a complete remasting, resparring, and rerigging—to restore the old frigate to sailing condition, but it is not a bad idea to ruminate about it. If the U.S. Congress were willing to spend enough money to restore and strengthen and reconstruct the ship to the noble state of sailing, it would not be an impossible dream. But then there would be hordes of nay-sayers. "Of what use would it be?" A good question—but there are several good answers. A seaworthy "Old Ironsides" might be of considerably more use than, say, Mount Rushmore. The ship is already a national monument, admittedly of less permanency than granite, but somehow more inspiring.

Constitution today is a deteriorating national monument; she is also a living symbol of our dauntless early Navy. A unique and symbolic monument, she has been there; it was her strength and power that impressed the mighty British Admiralty to order their naval commanders to avoid conflict

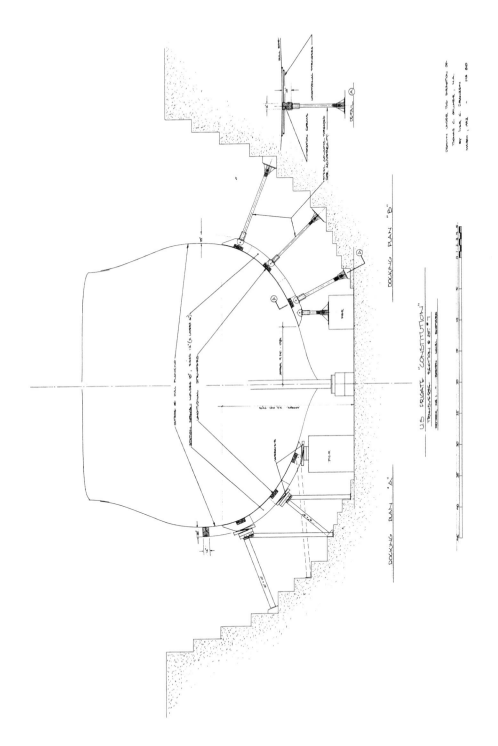

with American frigates. Hers was the strength and power that stopped the terrorism of lawless pirates of the Mediterranean—for a century and a half. "Old Ironsides," together with her few sisterships, stood against aggression on the sea in any form, and so established our country's first moves toward respect among nations. "Old Ironsides" is a symbol of these great American standards—and some of the brightest spots in our history.

Other values in this old, decaying ship are less visible. A large and straightforward, three-masted ship, she embodies very basic capabilities. For this reason, she was used in the 19th century as a school ship. So why not use her again for sail training of midshipmen? There are present-day educators and other self-appointed experts in naval training who would frown upon this idea, but I feel it has great merit, if for no other reason than to complement the current, nearly total academic study for budding naval officers.

In the complexities of modern technology and employment in today's workplace, whether aboard ship, in a business office, or elsewhere in organized society's working environment, the isolation is overwhelming. People become robotic, so completely absorbed in the immediate technical concentration of their individual work that the whole purpose of their contribution can be lost to them. Nowhere is this more evident than aboard a large ship—an aircraft carrier, a nuclear submarine, a missile cruiser. Whatever the vessel, individuals in small cubicles aboard one of these seagoing technological monsters, doing their cog-like thing, easily lose track of where they are. It is difficult for them to be conscious of being aboard a ship. Which is forward, which is aft? To port or to starboard? These may seem like minor things, yet they are major problems in the com-

Figure 5-8. A proposed system of bilge-support forms, with means for restorative pressure as required. Such apparatus would not be used without the removal of appropriate inner ceiling, stanchions, and other resistive structures; bottom plating and caulking would also be removed.

partmented "systems" environment provided in today's warships. It is a source of total disorientation—and, with it, insecurities and doubts—and even pyschological problems.

I believe, too, that much of the "systems" engineering theory and language has been overdone. It is time to downgrade it and allow us to emerge into a less dehumanized world. We can become better people when less dominated by such technology.

Before auxiliary mechanical propulsion of ships, when wind and sails moved ships, the shipboard environment was very simple. Every sailor was, first of all, a sailor. Only the cook and the captain did not stand watch. Wherever you are on board a sailing vessel, you know and are aware of where you are. It is clear what is going on and what your part is. Nobody aboard a sailing vessel—whether it is a large, three-masted, square-rigged frigate or a small schooner or sloop—is ignorant of which direction the ship is moving. Even if belowdecks, he knows forward from aft and port from starboard, and can hear the water as it rushes alongside.

And, until only about two decades ago, when officers and ratings and other sailors began to wear plastic nametags on their uniforms, it was assumed that they knew who they were. The custom of nametags has apparently become standard in all of the armed forces now—even the great General Schwarzkopf had to have his name patch sewn on his tropical uniform blouse in the 1991 war in the Gulf. Did the Army think no one would recognize him?

It is difficult to imagine Commodore Preble or Captain Isaac Hull or Lieutenant Stephen Decatur or even Lieutenants John F. Kennedy or George Bush wearing nametags. If this current practice is carried to its ultimate goal, only numbers will be needed.

All I am saying now is that we should make available a floating habitat like a great square-rigged ship to provide a learning opportunity in which all participants can know who they are—can know what they are doing and what they are contributing to the whole. On such a ship, people do not need to wear nametags; they are aware that the quality of their work, and their relationship with others will surely and more importantly establish their identity. When this awareness is generated among the crew of a sailing vessel, it becomes indelible.

It is an understatement to point out the great advantages of sail-training programs for enhancing and enabling the future of our young people. Such programs are needed, and there is none better in the development of self-confidence, self-esteem, and teamwork; there is no better way than living and working aboard a well-found sailing ship to know and acquire the values of dependability, credibility, and accountability, and all of the things that result in character.

It is my feeling that restoring *Constitution* to her sailing trim at the height of her career and using her as a school ship—in addition to passing on a respected national monument and symbol to the oncoming American generations—is something we should and can do with our deteriorating frigate "Old Ironsides," *our sole surviving frigate.*

Looking back, which is not always advisable, I can see that the pre-World War II Navy of the 1930s was closer to the Navy of 1812 than the Navy of today. It was a Navy without electronic wizardry, without rapid communication or even voice radio communication between ships. The propulsion plants, while powerful, were simple. No combined diesel/steam or diesel/electric (except submarines, which were separate things—surface diesel and submerged electric) existed; certainly no one could imagine nuclear power. The gunnery was gunpowder and shell; missiles were unheard of. Navigation without radar, without sonar, without satnav, was still the same old celestial observation: star sights, sun meridian altitude with plotted fixes after hand mathematical calculation. The use of sextant and compass and chronometer and lines of position were the only accepted navigational tools And nothing imparts the appreciation of the cosmos as sharply as nautical astronomy.

And the uniforms—have a look at the officer of the deck aboard the flagship of the Mediterranean squadron in 1936, checking the approach of an unexpected boat with the OD's telescope (Figure 5-9). This is not a cos-

Figure 5-9. Appearances aside, it was not too long ago—not 1812, 1850, or 1900, but only 1936—when this picture was taken of a U.S. naval officer doing his duty (officer of the deck) in dress uniform, aboard a Mediterranean flagship. The Navy of pre-World War II may have had more in common with the Navy of 1812–15 than with today's Navy. It was an austere Navy that stuck closely to the old traditions, even the early traditions—yet was credible enough to respond to the treacherous attack of the Japanese in 1941, push the war back to the very shores of Japan, and destroy their Imperial Navy.

tume for "HMS *Pinafore*"; it was the regular dress uniform for all officers, on Saturday morning inspections and/or official formalities. Captain Preble and Lieutenant Decatur would have been at ease on this Navy ship in 1936; John Paul Jones would have felt only a bit out of it. Our ship, USS *Raleigh*, had only six broadside guns (plus two two-gun turrets), but each fired a 90-pound, hand-loaded shell, by gun crews much the same as those on *Constitution*. We stripped to the waist and wore sweatbands around our heads and became loud and tough as powder and shell were passed to the first powderman, first loader, and rammer. The gun captain shouted "Bore clear" before each charge was rammed home, and the battery officer yelled "Fire"—not much different than on *Constitution*'s gun deck. The shipboard routine was the same; the boatswain on watch strode around the ship piping his pipe and passing the word. The quartermaster, at routine intervals, requested permission to wind and check the ship's chronometer. The lookout in the foremast top still announced a ship on the horizon with "Sail ho!" There was built-in respect for the opinion and decisions of others: the oncoming officer of the watch avoided making any change for 15 minutes, or until he had completely absorbed the ongoing conditions, course, weather, etc. This unwritten rule from the old ships, "Don't change the set of the sails for 15 minutes after relieving the watch," makes good general advice.

I think this is more than just nostalgia for the past. A sailing school ship is needed, perhaps more than one. The strongest point I can make is that, while it is not too late, the clock is ticking. And while it is ticking, the country is slogging along in a crippling economy. Differing structural proposals have been advanced toward solving the old frigate's restoration problems. The ingredient that is missing, unhappily, is the crank to start the engine. There seems to be no motivated individual or single-minded institution to carry the banner. Congress? Too busy with their personal and perpetual anxieties of reelection. The Navy Department? Too distracted with problems of demilitarization and new politics. *Constitution*'s historical supporters, be they organized or disorganized, are not of a single mind. Most potential supporters would plead the question of money and, sadly, this is the ultimate starter of the engine. But, finally, who will hoist the underway ensign?

There is the waiting, as the ship slips slowly away with only patchwork sustenance. She will not, as many youthful enthusiasts believe, live forever.

Epilogue, 1997

My study of *Constitution* and assessment of her structure began in 1991. I was asked by the Navy Department's Ship's Structures Division to provide not only an assessment of *Constitution*'s condition but also recommendations for correcting her longitudinal deformation and renewing her strength, which were considered to be impaired to an unknown but serious extent.

My most significant recommendation in this whole study and assessment was to stiffen *Constitution*'s bottom adjacent to her keel and backbone, extending outward and upward to her maximum breadth. It was her original designer and builder, Joshua Humphreys, who had recognized this need before construction and devised an inner structure—a rather radical procedure—to deal with it in his frigates. (A very similar plan, called the "Seppings System" after its creator Sir Robert Seppings, was devised some ten or fifteen years later for large warships of the British Navy.)

Humphreys called his system "diagonal riders," and his original description, which he signed, appeared in his document of specification for

44-gun frigates in 1794. It is known that these riders were installed on *Constitution*'s two sister ships. Humphreys also commented with considerable satisfaction on how well the riders worked in the frigate *United States* when she had a launching accident. However, there is no evidence of these riders being installed in *Constitution*. Nor is there any record of them being removed had she had them originally. There is early evidence of her keel being hogged, and there is also evidence of additional timbers—keel riders, sister keelsons, and such—having been added to do the work that the diagonal riders were meant to do. I strongly recommended that diagonal riders, closely following Humphreys' specifications, be installed.

Now it is 1997, and *Constitution* has been out of drydock for more than a year. She was refloated in the autumn of 1995, with her hull complete and strengthened with new diagonal riders, very well installed. The old frigate is very likely now to be stronger in her hull than at any time in the past 100 years or more. Her hull distortion has been essentially eliminated and her near-original shape is now locked in place.

Her drydockage was extended to allow for the very difficult inner hull work as well as other labor-intensive additions. Altogether she was out of her natural element for some three years, 1992 to 1995, and during this time, the diagonal rider installations were, no doubt, the most critical and important restorative work.

Regrettably, I cannot agree that some of the other new work is in any similar category. The most noticeable of the restoration work is the addition on the berth deck of some vertical-type, standing double-knees or perhaps standing knuckle knees. The names or definitive words are not available because there seems to be nothing historically similar.

These standing knuckle-like knees are actually a combination of standard (standing) and hanging knees. They are made up of laminated wood, so they become a combination of both, which gives the effect of massiveness. But, I feel, the added weight of these new forms contributes nothing to properly locating *Constitution*'s center of gravity, stability, or

Figure 1. The upper ends of a diagonal rider where it meets the underside of the berth deck. Altogether there are six pairs, port and starboard, bolted through the inner ceiling and outer planking (see Figure 5-5).

designed displacement. They add weight that will, in some amount, lessen the ship's transverse stability. Their structural contribution is questionable but they replace the essential hanging knees that existed in this part of the ship historically.

There is considerable replaced decking, and I must commend the director of this ship's restorative carpentry for some very skillful work. There are adjacent planks, called lock strakes, in the central portion of the decks

Figure 2. Combination standing and hanging knees. These newly invented shapes are laminated and thus have the virtue of not shrinking away from their tightly fitted bearing as the original hanging knees were inclined to do.

with rather unusual mortising to lock themselves together longitudinally. This sort of longitudinal locking system provides for a strake, or bands of decking, running continuously from stem to stern. I feel, as do some experienced shipbuilders, that this labor-intensive carpentry is redundant.

The mortised deck planks will, however, contribute interesting conversation pieces. As well will the new after standing knees against the transom.

Unlike the diagonal riders, these historically considered additions do not add measurable strength to the hull, though they do the ship no harm structurally.

Figure 3. "Lock strakes" in the decking, installed on both gun deck and berth deck. These mortises lock adjacent deck strakes together and provide the longitudinal strength of a wider plank.

Altogether we can be more than gratified that *Constitution*'s hull, despite the original hogging and other distortion, is now in excellent shape. Her planking below the waterline is sound. Her frames are also sound to a larger degree, and with the diagonal riders now in place, her hull will remain impervious to distortion for an indefinite time.

But to continue with an even more upbeat note, I wrote earlier that: "For her bicentennial summer of 1997 dare we expect that, with new sails and a well-trained crew, our country's original and only surviving frigate will once again move out and set her course down the harbor driven only by the wind?"

That statement now is no longer a wishful hope, it is an official promise. It is now the year of *Constitution*'s 200th birthday. Her sails are presently being made; the running rigging is being put in place. Commander Michael Beck, USN, the present commanding officer, is presiding over these and the many other necessary preparations to put the oldest surviving warship under sail.

The present operational plan, according to Commander Beck, is to proceed with the usual ceremony of the annual Fourth of July "turn around"—but with one difference. When the frigate is in the clear from the docks and piers, she will be cast free from the assisting tugboat, and she will spread her sails.

This first plan for sailing is to be historic (as well as economical). Sailing exercises are planned later in July. when tentative plans call for *Constitution* to sail coastwise, possibly near Gloucester and vicinity. She will set a first sail plan that I am sure she will have set many times before—a sail plan for battle and "general quarters" that both works well and is historically accurate. In such a plan no lower sails or courses are to be set—only the mizzen, the three topsails, and two jibs, and nothing higher. Such a sail plan allows full horizontal visibility and moderate speed under sail when approaching the enemy after the enemy ship is in desired range. This is the same sail plan *Constitution* carried in her overwhelming defeat of HMS *Guerriére* in 1812.

Crews are presently (winter of 1997) being trained for sailing aboard the replica of HMS *Bounty*, a contemporary of *Constitution* with a similar square rig. All these exercises and preparations certainly reinforce the promise of a renaissance of an existing national symbol, of national resolve against tyranny. What an exceptional and wonderful expectation!

Thomas C. Gillmer
Annapolis, Maryland
January 1997

Continuity of Aging

The Difference Between Restoration and Replacement

Speculation about how much original material is still in an old ship inevitably leads to the story of the "old battle axe" that has had three heads and four handles in its ten-score years. Is it still the original axe? In that case, the answer can be a firm "No!" An old ship, however, is an old ship even after much replacement of wood—but how much, and how extensive can it be? Are we discussing historic replacements, restorations, or reconstructions?

As discussed in Chapter Three, the case of the original frigate *Constellation* and the relic in Baltimore calling itself the same is the most well known—and perhaps politically controversial. While it is not closely relevant to the narrative of *Constitution*, it is of interest. First, because the two ships originally were designed by Joshua Humphreys and were part of the same six-warship authorization for the first U.S. Naval establishment. And now, the two ships—the claimed original *Constellation* in Baltimore and the *Constitution* in Boston—are so often publicly confused.

It apparently is not enough for a Navy office to release a publication of more than 200 pages based on more than two years of research (*Fouled Anchors: The* Constellation *Question Answered*; see Chapter Three) that refutes the *Constellation* society's claim. Nor to say that the Baltimore relic is an imposter. Perhaps a simpler, more graphic answer in this place will help.

The U. S. frigate *Constellation*, as was well documented by naval historian Howard Chapelle thirty years ago, ended her days and was cut up in pieces (recorded in the

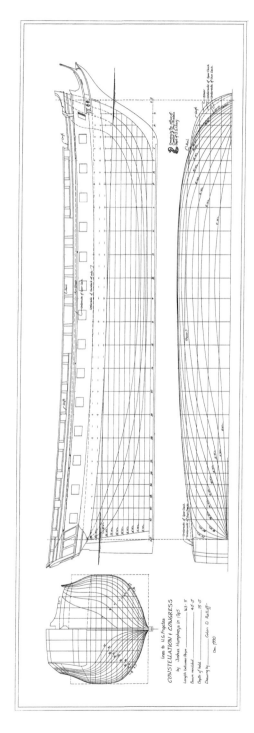

Figure 1. USS *Constellation*, designed by Joshua Humphreys in 1795, had a length between perpendiculars of 163 feet and a moulded beam of 40 feet.

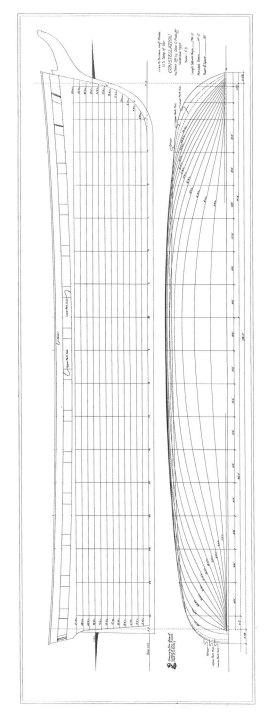

Figure 2. The USS *Constellation* of 1854 had a length between perpendiculars of 176 feet and a moulded beam of 41 feet.

Navy Yard's log) in Norfolk in 1853, at Gosport Navy Yard. There, in 1854, a new ship was launched, having been built 600 feet from the spot where the old *Constellation* was being destroyed. The new ship, which took the name USS *Constellation*, was not a frigate but a sloop-of-war—a warship then larger, but with one deck of guns. She was commissioned into the Navy July 28, 1855, and was the last sailing warship to enter the U. S. Navy. Designed by Chief Naval Constructor John Lenthall, she was not, as the Baltimore claimants insist, a "re-built," lengthened, and widened reconstruction using the same keel and original frame. The second *Constellation* was a *new* ship. The two ships, *Constitution* and *Constellation* as they exist today, reveal a different framing system. The original 1797 *Constellation* as designed by Humphreys had a framing system identical to that of *Constitution*. The framing of a ship is so fundamental that it cannot be changed, even in a major overhaul.

The records exist of the three different ships, their design, their construction. Records show also that one was destroyed and that two survive. The records show the three as being individually separate ships.

Herewith, the reader may look at the profiles of both *Constellation*s.

Humphreys's design shows a handsome frigate—smaller, but similar to *Constitution* and no less a masterful creation.

The profile in Figure 2 shows a ship longer, wider, deeper, and of greater freeboard with an elliptical stern—all features of ship styles of the 1850s, even with a much sharper entrance in the forward shape of the hull. The hollow sharpness in the water-lines is a likely adoption of clipper ship features so popular in the 1850s.

How much of *Constitution*'s original wood and timber is left? There are few records existing to make an accurate estimate. There have been many unfounded and even wild speculations that there is nothing left of her original hull, which is ridiculous. There is more of her original wood remaining than is generally believed.

Most of the original strength structure timber remains in her structural frame: the live oak frames and the white oak keel and keelson. This is the essence of a wooden ship.

Quoting from the *USS* Constitution *Maintenance Manual*:

3, 3, 3, FRAMES—

As the *Constitution*'s maintenance history indicates . . . removals and replacement of framing is a task that is seldom accomplished. In fact, all of the floors, most of the first futtocks and some of the second futtocks are original . . .

(Note: Most of the second futtocks reach as high as the gun deck and beyond, well above the load-waterline.)

Further—

Probably the most extensive amount of frame replacement ever undertaken in *Constitution*'s history was during the 1927–30 restoration. All of the framing from the third futtocks up was replaced, as were some of the first and second futtocks.

Since 1930, portions of the *Constitution*'s live oak framing have been replaced with laminated white oak. The new laminated sections were installed generally because of either rot in the live oak or excessive checking that left the wood incapable of holding a fastening.

Finally—

Unlike the case with planks or deck beams, there is really no such thing as a "minor repair" on the *Constitution*'s frames, since "repair" implies that a member is being restored to most of its original strength. The 20–25% of *Constitution*'s frames which incorporate short pieces have been significantly weakened. Unfortunately, scheduling and financial considerations have repeatedly inhibited past efforts to "do the job right" and resulted in the installation of these many short pieces of frame.

Building *Constitution*

Materials and Facilities

After Congress enacted the Naval Establishment into law on March 27, 1794, President George Washington referred the matter to his Secretary of War, Henry Knox.

Knox immediately called a conference of maritime-oriented gentlemen, which resulted in the call for ship designs and proposals. Joshua Humphreys submitted his designs and invited attention to the rather special features of his plans—not to be found in similar type frigates in navies of other nations. He pointed out that his designs showed three frigates of greater length, depth, and beam as well as greater sail area. They would carry greater firepower and have unusually heavy construction. They consequently would be able to engage or escape from any enemy at will. Further, due to the height of the gun-deck platform (8 feet) they would be able to engage two gun-deck ships when the latter would be forced to close their lower gun-deck ports in heavier weather.

Humphreys's philosophy of warship design was contained in a letter to Robert Morris, the government's finance minister who probably was much responsible for Humphreys getting the design contract for the six frigates.

Sir,—From the present appearance of affairs I believe it is time this country was possessed of a navy; but as that is yet to be raised, I have ventured a few remarks on the subject.

Ships that compose the European navys are generally distinguished by their rates; but as the situation and depth of water of our coasts and harbors are different in some degrees from those in Europe, and as our navy for a considerable time will be inferior in numbers, we are to consider what size ships will be most formidable, and be an overmatch for those of an enemy; such frigates in blowing weather would be an overmatch for double-deck ships, and in light winds to evade coming to action; or double-deck ships that would be an overmatch for common double-deck ships, and in blowing weather superior to ships of three decks, or in calm weather or light winds to outsail them. Ships built on these principles will render those of an enemy in a degree useless, or require a greater number before they dare attack our ships . . . As such ships will cost a large sum of money, they should be built of the best materials that could possibly be procured. . . .

The greatest care should be taken in the construction of such ships . . . for if we should be obliged to take a part in the present European war, or at a future day we should be dragged into a war with any powers of the Old Continent, especially Great Britain, they having such a number of ships of that size . . . it would be an equal chance by equal combat that we lose our ships. . . . Several questions will arise, whether one large or two small frigates contribute most to the protection of our trade, or which will cost the least sum of money, or whether two small ones are as able to engage a double-deck ship as one large one. For my part I am decidedly of opinion the large ones will answer best.

Joshua Humphreys

Building

The frigate *Constitution* was built at Hartt's Shipyard, Boston, during the years 1794–1797. She was launched after two unsuccessful attempts on October 21, 1797. Naval Constructor George Claighorne, USN, was in charge of construction. General Henry Jackson was naval agent and Captain Samuel Nicholson, inspector.

Suppliers

Gun carriages were built by Edmund Thayer.

Masts and spars, all of solid white pine, were cut at Unity, Maine, rolled and dragged to tidewater at Sheepscot River, Maine, and towed by packet to Boston.

Sails, of flax cloth, were made in Old Granary Building, Boston.

Carvings, bow and stern, and figurehead were by Skillins Brothers, Boston-New York.

Fastenings and metalwork were by Paul Revere, metalsmith, of Boston, who made all castings and forgings, rudder pintles, gudgeons, spikes, copper bolts, etc.

Rigging was by Cordwainers of Boston.

White oak timber was from Abbington and Merrimac Valley, Massachusetts, and Kennebec Valley, Maine.

Live oak timber was from Georgia Sea Islands, St. Simons, Blythe, Glover and Blackbeard. (Cost $16,000 for all six frigates.)

Yellow pine (long leaf) was from South Carolina and Georgia.

Note: *Constitution* had new masts fitted in 1811 that were built up and held tightly by woldings. These were installed in the Navy Yard, Boston.

APPENDIX III

Berth Deck—The Living Quarters

The berth deck plan in its current layout is an historic mix, with many 19th- and 20th-century features.

Beginning with the forward end of the ship, it is traditionally crews quarters, but it is not the traditional forecastle or foc's'l one normally expects—it wasn't from the beginning. A warship of this dimension, and a frigate, had a complement of approximately 450 men and officers. The officers did not live in the forward end, nor did any of the crew and ratings. Most of the crew swung in hammocks throughout the ship's waist. Look closely in Figure 4-7 at the deck beams above with the hammock hooks, closely spaced about 28–30 inches between. Navy ships were routinely fitted with hammock hooks on beams through World War II. Even the great Admiral Lord Nelson preferred to sleep in his specially constructed hammock.

On *Constitution* now, the crew aboard for its daily maintenance and routine, sleep on the deck below the berth deck, in specially fitted quarters and bunks on the orlop level.

The forward space is fitted as a "sick bay," the ship's quarters for the sick and physically disabled. There are four swinging cots or suspended single beds in the space, together with sanitary facilities. Just abaft the bulkhead separating the sick bay from the open portion of the berth deck is the ship's brig.

The open quarters of the berth deck in the forward half contain sea chests along both sides, and the two large hatches for vertical access along the center. There are various accommodation facilities, such as the warrant officers pantry, work bench, chests, etc.

In the after portion of this deck level are primarily the midshipmen's and officers' quarters. On the port side aft are the staff officers' staterooms. First in line are the ship's carpenter and sailmaker's quarters respectively, followed by the warrant officers' mess room and next is the larger, but not necessarily more significant, junior watch midshipmen's mess. These spaces are followed by sailing master, purser, surgeon, chaplain, marine officer, and finally the secretary. It is interesting to compare these officers' spaces and their apparent ranking seniority. (Ranking, because, as the rooms proceed toward the stern they necessarily, along the outboard side, become successively smaller.) The sailing master is of ranking importance. While not of a commissioned rank, he was of significance on the quarter deck between the captain and the first lieutenant. His advice and directions in sailing were a tactical necessity. He probably relates most closely in modern hierarchy to the chief engineer. Both titles are responsible for the ship's propulsive system.

On the starboard or ranking side of the ship are arranged the commissioned line officers' quarters. These follow the purser's issuing room and the two small staterooms for the gunner and the boatswain, which are separated from the officers' row by the midshipmen's senior watch room. The officers' row of staterooms begins with the first lieutenant's. This officer is second in line command of the ship and in modern identity is the executive officer. The name of this office is an historic inheritance from the old British system of ranking when there were no other named ranks between captain and the lieutenants below him. Consequently, the staterooms remain on *Constitution* for first lieutenant through sixth lieutenant on the starboard side. None of these are especially comfortable quarters for comparable standing in command sequence on a modern warship.

In the center section between the officers' and staff cabins is the large wardroom. This is the larger, more comfortable lounge and dining room where all the officers found their relaxation. This is the locale of the highest and lowest of the ship's leadership, rather like a private club presided over by the first lieutenant (executive officer nowadays). There are two dining tables, probably divided between the senior and junior officers, both served from the same pantry, which is in the stern just below the transom and the tiller. It must have been a hazardous place in heavy weather.

The arrangement described above is more or less the historic plan. It must be remembered again, the long active service of this ship and its various commands and employments. It is not exactly as it was originally or at any one given period in its aging life. But also keep in mind that *this* deck below the gun deck was the "living" deck. It was not where the "cannons roared" nor was it the deck once "red with heroes' blood." But this is rather the deck where former heroes lived and slept; the young

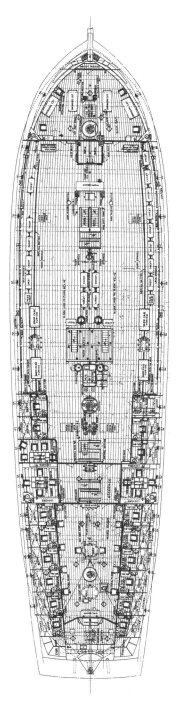

Figure 1. Berth deck arrangement as rendered by John Lord for the 1927–1930 restoration.

officers who freed the captive frigate *Philadelphia* from its terrorist captors, and the many hundreds who manned the guns that destroyed the *Guerrière* and other British ships conquered by "Old Ironsides." It is the deck where midshipmen lived and studied when she was a school ship. It is also the deck that became a filthy stable for the livestock of Captain Jesse Elliot, who believed *Constitution* to be his private transport and farm. It is a place that is full of human American history—both great and small.

APPENDIX IV

Wood for Ship's Structures

The more time between now and the end of the days of wooden ships, the greater the extent of our ignorance of wood shipbuilding—much knowledge has gone. Although there are attempts to keep the literature alive, they are few and isolated. Such publications as *WoodenBoat* are most commendable, but they deal only with *small* boat construction. Building a large vessel in wood is something else. The handling of the heavy timber in ships requires a special knowledge that is not very marketable. It requires an intimate knowledge of wood species and wood properties—a close understanding of the chemistry of wood and its physical reactions to atmospheric changes. Such scientific knowlege perhaps exceeds the range of working knowledge of old-time ship builders, but what we must learn today to build a wooden ship is available; not historically, but only scientifically and empirically. Old-time shipbuilders acquired their skill and knowledge from uncounted years of tradition and experience.

Ships of wood have been built from the beginning. We will not know how many or for how long. We know that as human populations grew and cultures expanded, so did the number of ships and their size. It was a proportional expansion—wooden ships became larger and more complex. They served to support trade, become vehicles for the ages of discovery, colonization, and the resulting conflicts among nations. Whole geographic areas such as the Aegean islands and the forests of Lebanon were denuded of trees in antiquity to build warships. It required perhaps 200 large trees to build an Athenian trireme in 500 B.C. So how many trees were involved in supporting the westward expansive campaign of Xerxes and his Persian hordes when his ships took on the Athenians at the Battle of Salamis? This greedy dictator brought over 600 ships against the Greeks' 200 triremes. They were all similar sized galleys—approximately 36 meters (118 feet) long. Nearly 2,000 years later the greater galleys of the Venetian states and those of the Genoese were larger. And to that add the galleons and other warships of the Dutch, the Spanish, and the English that supported their East India trades as well as western world exploitations. And the great ships-of-the-line of Nelson's Navy and his enemies were massive wooden machines. A 74-gun ship could well have taken 1,500 mature trees to provide its wooden frame and structure. An oak tree large enough to be shaped into a keel timber for USS *Constitution* ($24'' \times 18''$) must have been 175 to 200 years old. There are no trees growing in Europe large enough to support even a small wooden ship flotilla today.

Wood species used in shipbuilding

In selecting and preparing the "right" wood the right way for the many applications in a large wooden vessel, the advice from old salts and Downeasters has become almost holy writ. But the advice is old and comes down from time-warped sources.

We can separate the wheat from the chaff by reading the shipbuilding contracts from the old records where the type of ship and the kind of wood is plainly set down. This can be and sometimes necessarily is modified by the availability of wood today. The original specifications for USS *Constitution* clearly stated the wood species. For the better-quality ships in America of the late 18th and the 19th centuries the frame and backbone were most frequently oak. White oak for the keel, keelson, stem, and sternposts, and live oak for the frames. The live oak is technically a type of white oak growing in southern North America, particularly in coastal areas of the South Atlantic states. It develops large lower branches and large roots near the surface. These curving limbs produce natural curves of timber that can be selected for the various transverse curvatures in the frames, knees, and deadwood crooks.

The white oak used in the planking as well as that in the straight timbers of the keel and keelson was taken from oaks that grew in timber stands or forest oak. These were the trees forced by their location to reach for the sky and sun, and have beautiful runs of straight grain unmarked or uninterrupted by the intervention of the circular growth of branched trunks. Lengths of 40 to 50 feet of straight-growth planks as well as heavier timber lengths were, and are, possible. These oaks—the traditional high-quality hardwoods for shipbuilding—historically have been available in the eastern United States.

In the softwood category shipbuilding demands point first to Douglas-fir. This multipurpose wood was used in deck beams as an alternative to oak, and frequently used in decking and in lower mast sections—either solid spar in the smaller masts or built-up in cored sections for the larger masts exceeding 24 inches in diameter. For the upper masts and spars, spruce—the most desirable of which was Sitka spruce—was used because of its long straight growth, flexible strength, and low density.

Varying species of wood was necessary when the ship's center of gravity control was considered—heavy woods low and lighter woods above and aloft. Although white oak is not a particularly heavy wood among hardwoods, it is approximately 30% heavier than Douglas-fir and 40% heavier than Sitka spruce. These weight differences accumulate to become significant in a ship's structure.

Current availability of shipbuilding wood

This brief discussion of wood is to this point based on historic concepts and American tradition. Nothing has been said about wood from other countries. Of course, historically, American shipbuilders feasted in American forests—as did European shipbuilders in the late 18th century, particularly the British Naval shipyards. The growing scarcity of wood in England and the closing of many European sources because of protracted wars forced the British to rely on American colonies. Their timber ships spent much time loading timber from northern New England and Canada.

Now we find our own sources are narrowing as our knowledge of tropical hardwoods increases. Confined in the past to exotic woods for furniture, and focusing mostly on mahogany and teak of the Far East, this knowledge has led to the forests of Central and South America. Wooden shipbuilding in the United States or elsewhere is not going to denude any country's hillsides nowadays or in the future. Politically and ecologically it would be far better to encourage *limited* harvest of fine tropical forest growth rather than the devastating random destruction of trees that is currently proceeding in Brazil and other Latin American countries. There is wood whose properties far exceed the qualities of North American oaks and firs. Woods whose density is more than twice that of white oak. Most all of the tropical hardwoods are rot or decay resistant to a greater extent than teak. This wood is most valuable for alternatives to oak in shipbuilding and it is available.

Domestically, how available is white oak? It is available, and sporadically it can be obtained in the longer lengths of straight unobstructed grain of the highest quality. The builders of *Pride Of Baltimore II* obtained eighty prime white oaks, for example, from a highway department making way for another road. The cost was only that for milling the trees into 2½ inch planking stock or to other necessary dimensions.

Figure 1. Dressing down the heavy hardwood to its final sided dimension. A powered hand planer does this job more efficiently and accurately than the old hand planes. It still remains a task for only the skillful shipwright.

Figure 2. A finished keel timber section with a scarf ready to receive the lower stem section. This wood is a tropical hardwood, called Cortez, from Belize, in Central America. Its specific gravity is 1.15, near that for Lignum Vitae, historically the heaviest and hardest of woods. It will remain very stable dimensionally, resist decay, and turn away the teredo (ship worms and borers).

Seasoned wood and moisture content

Many self-styled boatbuilding experts—most of whom have never built a boat or a ship—have developed formulas and rules of thumb about air dried versus kiln dried, or how long or how many years per inch or inches per year it takes to "season." All of these undocumented rules are rather undependable. There are many, many variables that affect the drying or "seasoning" or the control of the moisture content of wood: humidity, temperature, the cellular structure of the wood, and the moisture content at the beginning are only a few.

It may cause despair in the hallowed chambers of traditional thought on wooden boat and ship construction that most wooden ships of the past and some of the better ones in recent years have used much wood directly from the forest sawmills. I recall opening a sealed ship's container from Belize, packed with tropical woods for a ship's structure, and feeling and smelling the jungle moisture that flowed out. The timber, only partially milled on the site where it was felled, was visibly wet with condensation. One could almost hear the screaming monkeys and the calls of parrots.

Figure 3. A timber finished on both sides (sided to dimension); it will be sawn to the pattern shape for the "gripe," a lower stem knee. The wood is a tropical hardwood called bulit tree—very decay resistant, high density, and worm resistant. The heart wood can be seen beneath the shipwright's pattern.

Figure 4. The scarf in the forward keel section will fit into that of the keel timber in Figure 2.

It should not be inferred that the moisture content of wood should be ignored—it should be closely accounted for and dealt with. Where white oak is used for the ship's planking it will be necessarily subjected to the high temperatures of a tight steam box, which thoroughly cleanses the cellular structure of the wood, rendering it more supple for bending to place on a ship's frame. Most planking will receive 3 to 6 hours in the steam box. On larger, thicker planking, steaming may not be enough for dealing with the quicker curves and bending. *Constitution*'s planking was boiled in deep tanks before it was applied.

The heavier wood of the keel and the stern- and stemposts—which will be below the waterline and long saturated—is either straight, needing no bending, or sawn to shape.

While the ship's structure is being assembled outside in the sun and weather, a builder should try to maintain a stable moisture content. It is best, particularly during the summer building months, to keep it shaded and treat it with a surface coating of preservative paint or a reflective paint. The exposed ends of timbers are most susceptible to breathing moisture in and out, and should be sealed.

The following table provides the weights and specific gravities of various species of wood, both green and saturated, as well as the preferable 15% moisture content for the stable working value.

AVERAGE WEIGHT PER CUBIC FOOT FOR VARIOUS WOODS UNDER DIFFERENT MOISTURE CONTENT CONDITIONS AND SPECIFIC GRAVITY BASED ON WEIGHT WHEN OVEN-DRY AND VOLUME WHEN GREEN

Species	Weight per Cubic Foot			
	Specific Gravity	Green	15% Moisture Content	Oven-dry
HARDWOODS				
Angelique	0.60	67	46	44
Apitong	.58	—	44	41
Ash:				
Black	.45	55	35	33
Green	.53	—	41	38
Oregon	.50	—	38	36
White	.55	50	42	40
Basswood, American	.32	36	25	24
Beech, American	.56	54	44	42
Birch, Yellow	.55	60	43	41
Cherry, Black	.47	46	36	33
Elm, Rock	.57	51	44	41
Greenheart	.81	—	61	56
Hickory:				
Mockernut	.64	68	50	49
Pignut	.66	70	52	50
Shagbark	.64	—	50	48
Shellbark	.62	—	49	48
Iroko	.55	—	40	36
Ironbark, Gray	1.00	—	—	62
Khaya ("African Mahogany")	.43	—	32	29
Lauan, Red	.40	—	31	28
Lignumvitae (Guaiacum spp.)	1.20	—	76	—

Species	Specific Gravity	Weight per Cubic Foot		
		Green	15% Moisture Content	Oven-dry
Locust:				
Black	.66	—	50	46
Honey	.63	—	48	44
Mahogany (Swietenia spp.)	.45	—	34	30
Maple:				
Black	.52	—	40	38
Sugar	.56	58	43	41
Maria	.50	—	39	37
Oak:				
Red Oaks:				
Black	.56	—	43	41
Northern Red	.56	63	43	40
Pin	.58	—	44	42
Scarlet	.60	—	46	43
Southern Red	.52	59	41	39
White Oaks:				
Bur	.58	—	44	40
Chestnut	.57	—	45	43
Live	.81	—	63	59
White	.60	61	47	44
Okoume (Gaboon)	.35	—	27	25
Pecan	.60	—	46	43
Peroba do campo	.69	—	63	58
Sweetgum	.46	52	36	34
Tangile	.53	—	41	38
Teak	.58	—	43	39
Walnut, Black	.51	60	39	37
Yellow Poplar	.40	46	31	28
SOFTWOODS				
Bald Cypress	.42	58	32	29

Species	Weight per Cubic Foot			
	Specific Gravity	Green	15% Moisture Content	Oven-dry
Cedar:				
Alaska	.42	35	32	29
Atlantic White	.31	—	23	21
Eastern Redcedar	.44	37	33	30
Incense	.35	32	26	24
Northern White	.20	—	21	19
Port Orford	.40	37	30	28
Western Redcedar	.31	31	23	21
Douglas-fir:				
Coast	.45	38	34	32
Intermediate	.41	34	31	29
Rocky Mountain	.40	32	30	28
Larch, Eastern (Tamerack, Hackmatack)	.49	36	30	28
Larch, Western	.51	49	39	37
Pine:				
Eastern White	.34	—	25	23
Loblolly	.47	39	36	33
Longleaf	.54	44	41	38
Ponderosa	.38	33	28	26
Shortleaf	.46	38	35	33
Slash	.56	—	43	40
Sugar	.35	43	27	25
Western White	.36	36	27	25
Redwood	.38	44	28	25
Spruce:				
Red (Eastern)	.38	32	29	27
Sitka	.37	33	28	26
White (Eastern)	.37	—	28	27

The weight per cubic foot includes both the weight of the dry wood substance and the water.

Values given apply to heartwood, not sapwood (near the bark).

Tabular values above are from *Wood: A Manual for Its Use as a Shipbuilding Material*, Department of the Navy.

APPENDIX V

Constitution's Contemporary and Companion Vessels

What follows are twelve design drawings in lines profile, body, and half-breadth of frigates, ships, brigs, and schooners that sailed in that first and early U.S. Navy through the War of 1812. *Constitution* was authorized and built at the same time as some, sailed as flagship in the same squadron as some, and was contemporary with all during their lifetimes. They are described, not chronologically but individually, with their dates and places of construction, builders and designers, principal dimensions, and other definitive remarks. These architectural drawings are photocopied directly from the originals and are part of the official Naval Documents as ordered by President Franklin D. Roosevelt and authorized by Congress in March 1934. These are from the volumes covering the Barbary Wars, 1801–1807.

Note: The *Wasp* (Plate 10) was first designed to be a brig, and she was launched this way. Later, before commissioning, Josiah Fox made some alterations, changing *Wasp* to a ship-rigged sloop of war, as shown in Plate 11. Instead of a brig's two masts she has the three masts of the ship. Her channels are moved from just above the mainwale, which was proper design, to the caprail of the bulwarks. Decorated quarter galleries were also added. In Chapelle's *American Sailing Navy*, he explains the change in height of the channels. Because they were just below the gunport sills, they "would have been in the way for sweeps and would have endangered boarding." This is a reasoning difficult to understand. In the original design the channels were located very much according to the usual placement. The idea that they would interfere with sweeps and with boarding ease sounds a little contrived.

Vixen (Plate 9) is a design attributed to Benjamin Hutton of Philadelphia. No doubt Hutton is responsible for the handsome design drawings and the necessary design technology, but she was built in Baltimore by William Price. Mr. Price was known as others in the Fells Point Yards as a Baltimore Clipper builder. The design profiles and body of *Vixen* show this influence reflected in the handsome little schooner.

Altogether, these original design drawings exhibit a sampling of our original Navy. All of these vessels have a typical American style, and show at the same time technological advance when compared to European vessels of the same time.

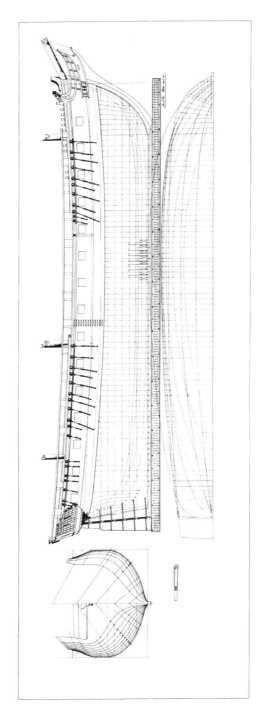

Constitution, Frigate, 44 guns.

Built at Boston under Act of Congress, March 27, 1794. Cost $302,719. Designed by Joshua Humphreys. Agent: Henry Jackson. Builder: George Claighorn. Launched: October 21, 1797. Commissioned July 2, 1798. Carvings by John and S. Skillen from designs by William Rush.

Principal dimensions: Length on main deck (Gun Deck)—175'; Breadth—44'6"; Depth—14'3"; Tonnage—1,576; Complement—400. Battery (1804)—30 24-pounders, 14 12-pounders, and 8 32-pound carronades.

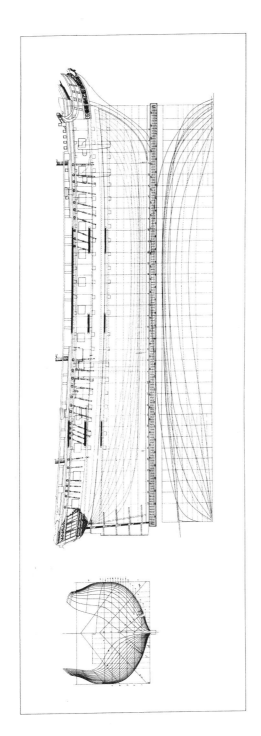

Constellation, Frigate, 36 guns.

Built at Baltimore under Act of Congress, March 27, 1794. Cost $314,212. Designed by Joshua Humphreys. Agent: S. & J. Sterrett. Builder: David Stodder. Launched: September 7, 1797. Commissioned June 26, 1798. Carvings by William Rush.

Principal dimensions: Length on deck—162′10″; Breadth—41′2″; Depth—18′9″; Tonnage—1,278; Complement—320; Battery (1800)—28 18-pounders, 10 24-pound carronades.

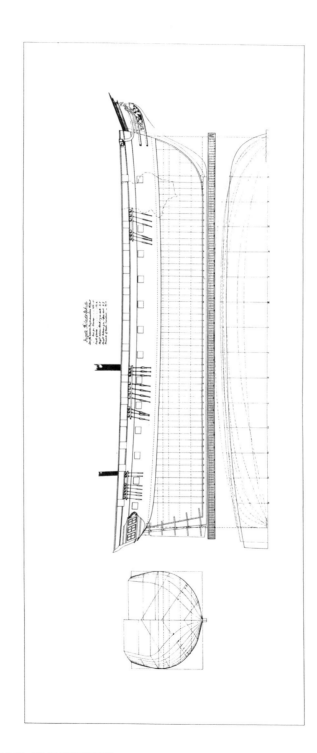

Philadelphia, Frigate, 36 guns.
Built at Philadelphia for U.S. Government by citizens of Philadelphia under Act of Congress, June 30, 1798. Cost $179,349. Designed by Josiah Fox. Builders: Samuel Humphreys, Nathaniel Hutton, and John Delavue. Launched: November 28, 1799. Commissioned April 5, 1800. Carvings by William Rush.
Principal dimensions: Length of keel—130'; Breadth—39'; Depth—13'6"; Tonnage—1,240; Complement—307; Battery (1803)—28 18-pounders, 16 32-pounders, 16 32-pound carronades.

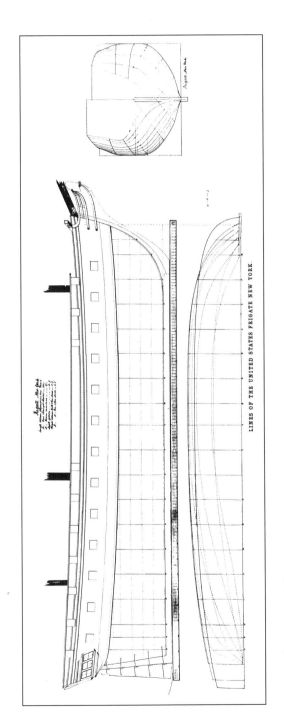

LINES OF THE UNITED STATES FRIGATE NEW YORK.

New York, Frigate, 36 guns.

Built at New York for U.S. Government by citizens of New York under Act of Congress, June 30, 1798. Cost $159,639. Designed by Samuel Humphreys. Builder: Peck and Carpenter. Launched: April 24, 1800. Commissioned October 30, 1800. Carvings, unknown sculptor.

Principal dimensions: Length on deck—145 ′5 ″; Breadth—38 ′1 ″; Depth—11 ′9 ″; Tonnage—not available; Complement—340; Battery (1799)—26 18-pounders, unknown number of 9 pounders.

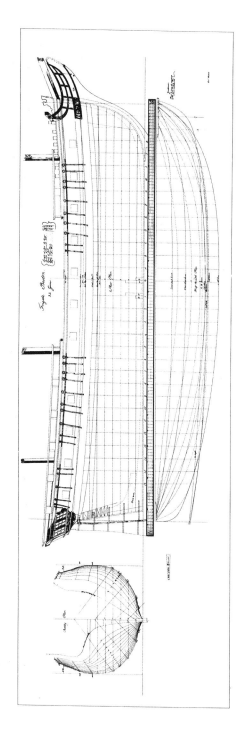

Boston, Frigate, 28 guns.

Built at Boston for U.S. Government by citizens of Boston under Act of Congress, June 30, 1798. Cost $119,570. Designed by Edmund Hartt. Built by Edmund Hartt. Launched May 20, 1799. Commissioned July 24, 1799. Principal dimensions: Length on deck—133′; Breadth—35′6″; Depth—17′11″; Tonnage—not available; Complement—220; Battery (1801)—26 12-pounders, 6 9-pounders, 12 32-pound carronades.

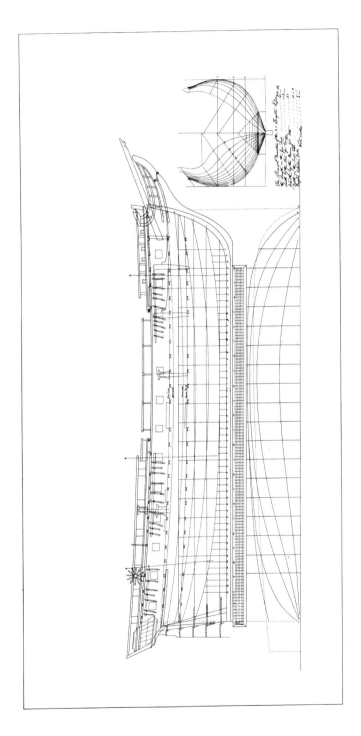

Essex, Frigate, 32 guns.
Built at Salem, Massachusetts, for U.S. Government by citizens of Salem under Act of Congress, June 30, 1798. Cost $139,362. Designed by William Hackett. Agent: Joseph Waters. Builder: Enos Briggs. Launched September 30, 1799. Commissioned December 17, 1799. Carvings by Samuel McIntire.
Principal dimensions: Length on gun deck—141′5″; Breadth—37′8″; Depth—12′3″; Tonnage—850; Complement—228; Battery (1799)—26 12-pounders, 10 6-pounders.

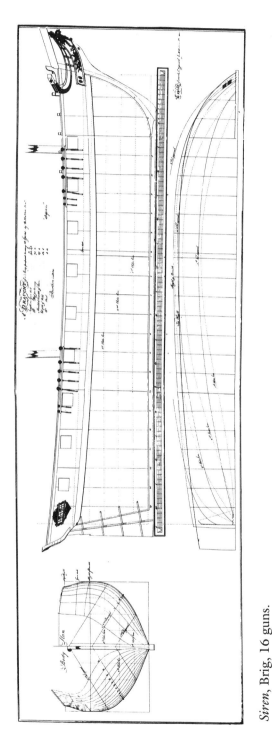

Siren, Brig, 16 guns.
Built at Philadelphia under Act of Congress, February 23, 1803. Cost $32,522. Designed by Benjamin Hutton. Agent: George Harrison. Builder: Nathaniel Hutton. Launched August 8, 1803. Commissioned on or about September 1, 1803. Principal dimensions: Length on main deck—94′6″; Breadth—27′9″; Depth—12′6″; Tonnage—240; Complement—120; Battery (1803)—16 24-pound carronades.

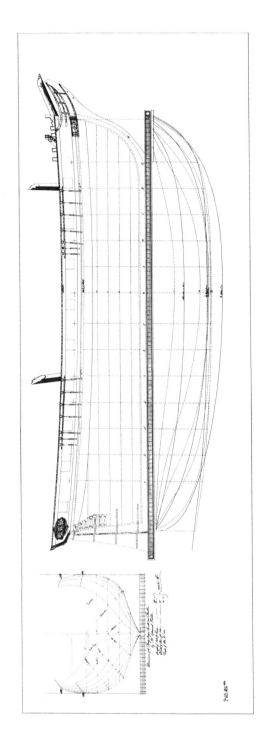

Argus, Brig, 18 guns.

Built at Boston under Act of Congress February 23, 1803. Cost $37,428. Designed by Joseph Hartt. Agent: Samuel Brown. Builder: Edmund Hartt. Launched August 21, 1803. Commissioned September 6, 1803. Principal dimensions: Length on deck—95′10″; Breadth—28′2″; Depth—12′8″; Tonnage—not available; Complement—142; Battery (1803)—16 24-pound carronades.

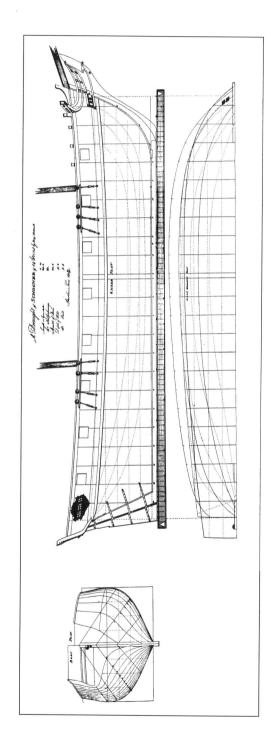

Vixen, Schooner (later Brig), 12 guns.
Built at Baltimore under Act of Congress, February 23, 1803. Cost $20,872. Designed by Benjamin Hutton. Agent: John Stricker. Builder: William Price. Launched June 25, 1803. Commissioned August 3, 1803.
Principal dimensions: Length on gun deck—84'0"; Breadth—23'8"; Depth 9'6"; Tonnage—170; Complement—111; Battery (1803)—12 18-pound carronades.

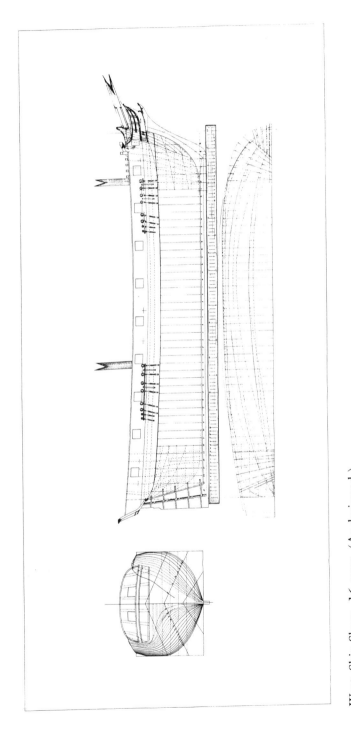

Wasp, Ship Sloop, 16 guns. (As designed.)
Built at Washington Navy Yard, under Act of Congress, March 26, 1804. Cost not available. Designed by Josiah Fox.
Builder: Josiah Fox. Launched April 21, 1806. Commissioned May 1, 1807.
Principal dimensions: Length (between perp.)—105′; Breadth—30′11″; Depth—14′1″; Tonnage—450; Complement—
140; Battery (1807)—16 32-pound carronades, 2 12-pounders.

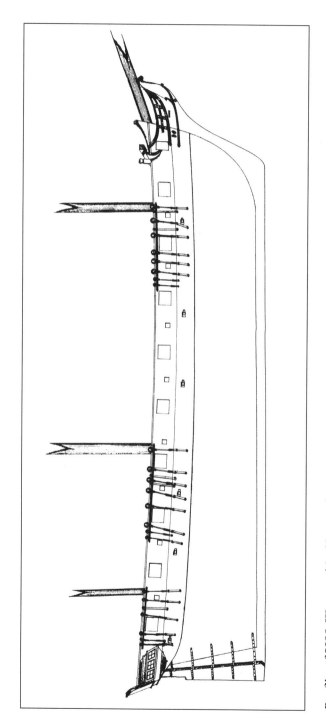

Profile of USS *Wasp* as ship (3 masts).

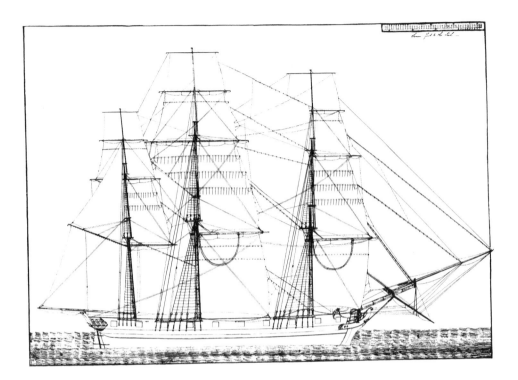

Sail plan profile of USS *Wasp*.

ENDNOTES

CHAPTER 1

1. "Weight" of a naval gun was expressed in the weight of the spherical iron projectile it fired (the cannonball).
2. These upper light sails were probably not carried until after 1803.

CHAPTER 2

1. Hyde's story appeared in the July 22, 1812, edition of the *Maryland Republican*.

CHAPTER 3

1. Four 74-gun ships-of-the-line had been authorized during the War of 1812: *Franklin, Columbus, Washington,* and *Independence.* Although *Columbus* and *Franklin* met expectations, these first two were not considered quite good enough for the 1816 Congressional resolution for naval expansion. Until the new 74s were built, the tried-and-true 44-gun frigates continued to prevail.
2. Spencer gaffs were added to the fore and main for lower fore-and-aft sails.
3. The naval records for this important overhaul period, which include the original

correspondence between Captain Morris, the superintendent of the Charlestown Navy Yard at Boston, and his superior, Captain John Rodgers, the presiding officer of the Navy Board of Commissioners in Washington, are currently missing from the naval document files in the National Archives. At this writing, there is no explanation for this situation. We can only assume that some researcher in the past has removed these letters for reasons unknown. The records for the time period immediately prior and immediately following are in place. The very valuable knowledge of what actually was accomplished in 1833–34 during this first major overhaul and restoration must remain unknown.

4. Frames are the rib-like members that are fundamental to the ship's structure. After laying the keel, the frames are placed and fastened on top of the keel, giving the ship its form and three-dimensional geometry. Frame locations and spacing are determined by the ship's design and cannot be changed without destroying the ship.

5. CSS *Virginia*.

CHAPTER 4

1. "Who Designed 'Old Ironsides'?," by William Bass. *Naval History*, Vol. 5, No. 2. U.S. Naval Institute Press.

CHAPTER 5

1. *Essai Geometrique et Pratique sur L'Architecture Navale*, by M. Vial du Clairbois, Paris: 1776.

SOURCES AND REFERENCES

Beverly R. Robinson Collection of Naval Prints
    U. S. Naval Academy, Segrid Trumpy, Curator
    Annapolis, Maryland

Boarders Away
    by William Gilkerson
    1991, Andrew Mobray, Inc., Lincoln, Rhode Island

"*Constellation* Evidence and Warship Design"
    by Colan Ratliff
    from *Fouled Anchors: The* Constellation *Question Answered*; 1991, David Taylor
    Research Center, U.S. Navy
    Bethesda, Maryland

Fouled Anchors: The Constellation *Question Answered*
    by Dana M. Wegner
    1991, David Taylor Research Center, U.S. Navy
    Bethesda, Maryland

The History of the American Sailing Navy
    by Howard I. Chapelle
    1949, W. W. Norton & Co., New York

A Most Fortunate Ship, A Narrative History of Old Ironsides
    by Tyrone G. Martin, Captain, USS *Constitution*
    1980, The Globe Pequot Press, Chester, Connecticut

Naval Documents (Related to the) United States Wars with the Barbary Powers, etc.
    1939, Office of Naval Records, U.S. Navy Department

The Peabody Museum of Salem
    Photography Curator, Kathy Flynn
    Salem, Massachusetts

Recueil de Petites Marines
    by Jean-Jerome Baugean, Graveur du Roi
    1817 a Paris, Chez Ostewald aine
    1987 Facsimile by le Chasse-Maree

A Short History of the United States Navy
    by Carroll S. Alden, Ph.D.
    Head, Department of History, U.S. Naval Academy
    1927, J. B. Lippincott Co., Philadelphia

To Shining Sea, A History of the United States Navy
    by Stephen Howarth
    1991, Random House, New York

Donald S. Turner, Maintenance Superintendent
    USS *Constitution*, Boston Navy Yard

United States Archives
    Washington, D. C.

U. S. Naval Academy Museum
    James Cheevers, Curator
    Annapolis, Maryland

United States Naval Institute, Photographic Library
    Patty M. Maddock, Director
    U. S. Naval Academy
    Annapolis, Maryland

U. S. Navy Photographic Center
    Commanding Officer, U. S. Naval Station
    Washington, D. C.

"Who Designed 'Old Ironsides'?"
    by William Bass. *Naval History*, Vol. 5, No. 2. U.S.
    Naval Institute Press

ILLUSTRATION CREDITS

Chapter-opening illustrations and color insert: William Gilkerson.

CHAPTER 1

Figures 1-1 and 1-2: Thomas C. Gillmer; Figures 1-3 and 1-4: National Archives; Figures 1-5 and 1-6: Thomas C. Gillmer; Figure 1-7: U.S. Navy; Figures 1-8 through 1-11: *Steel's Elements of Mastmaking, Sailmaking, and Rigging.*

CHAPTER 2

Figure 2-1: Jean Jerome Baugean, Recueil de Petits Marines; Figure 2-2: U.S. Navy, Office of Naval Records; Figures 2-3 and 2-4: Jean Jerome Baugean, Recueil de Petits Marines; Figure 2-5: U.S. Navy, Office of Naval Records; Figure 2-6: Jean Jerome Baugean, Recueil de Petits Marines; Figures 2-7 and 2-8: Jean Jerome Baugean, Batimens de Guerre; Figures 2-9 through 2-11: Jean Jerome Baugean, Recueil de Petits Marines; Figure 2-12: Thomas C. Gillmer; Figure 2-13: U.S. Navy, Office of Naval Records; Figure 2-14: U.S. Naval Academy; Figure 2-15: U.S. Navy, Office of Naval Records; Figures 2-16 and 2-17: Peabody Museum, Salem, Massachusetts;

Figures 2-18 and 2-19: Jean Jerome Baugean, Robinson Collection, U.S. Naval Academy; Figure 2-20: Robinson Collection, U.S. Naval Academy; Figure 2-21: Jean Jerome Baugean, Robinson Collection, U.S. Naval Academy; Figure 2-22: Thomas C. Gillmer.

CHAPTER 3

Figure 3-1: USNI; Figure 3-2: Frederic S. Cozzens; Figure 3-3: Capt. H. Cassidy, USN, Ret.; Figures 3-4 through 3-8: USNI.

CHAPTER 4

Figure 4-1: Capt. H Cassidy, USN, Ret.; Figure 4-2: Thomas C. Gillmer; Figure 4-3: Donald S. Turner, U.S. Navy Repair and Maintenance, Navy Yard, Boston; Figures 4-4 through 4-11: Thomas C. Gillmer; Figure 4-12: USNI; Figure 4-13: Thomas C. Gillmer.

CHAPTER 5

Figures 5-1 through 5-3: Thomas C. Gillmer; Figure 5-4: Capt. H. Cassidy, USN, Ret.; Figure 5-5: Thomas C. Gillmer; Figures 5-6 and 5-7: USNI; Figures 5-8 and 5-9: Thomas C. Gillmer.

EPILOGUE

Figures 1, 2, and 3: Thomas C. Gillmer.

APPENDIX I

Figures 1 and 2: Colan D. Ratliff.

APPENDIX III

Figure 1: John Lord, USNI.

APPENDIX IV

Figures 1 through 4: Thomas C. Gillmer.

APPENDIX V

U.S. Government Printing Office.

INDEX